Copyright © 2012 Jo Franks

Table of Contents

Table of Contents iii
Preface vi

Chapter 1

A-M 1

Algerian Lamb Shanks with Cardamom and Orange 1
Arni Lemonato (Roast Lemon Lamb) 2
Asian Crepinettes 3
Basic Kibbi 4
Beef Or Lamb Baked With Yogurt And Black Pepper 5
Bharwaan Dum Ki Raan 6
Bhunawa Salan 8
Bichak (Stuffed Baked Tricorners) 9
Braised Lamb Shanks with Roasted Potatoes 12
Braised Lamb Shanks with White Beans 14
Braised Lamb Shoulder with Figs 15
Broiled Lamb Chops With Braised Root Vegetables, Colcannon .. 17
Burgoo 18
Butterflied Leg of Lamb 20
Carnero En Adobe – Tangy Braised Lamb Shanks 22
Chappal Kebab – Hamburger Kebabs 23
Chicken Or Lamb Biryani 24
Chili With Lamb And Black Beans 25
Cocktail Kabobs 27
Dingle Pie 28
Dolmades (Stuffed Grape Leaves) 30
Easy Lamb Creole Gumbo 31
Feta And Black Olive Crusted Roasted Leg Of Lamb 32
French Onion Lamb Au Jus 34
Fruit-Braised Lamb Shanks 34
Gigot D'agneau Boneless Leg Of Lamb 36
Hammin Di Pesach (lamb, Meatballs & Spinach For Passover) ... 36

Herb Crusted Leg Of Lamb	38
Indian Braised Lamb	39
Indian Mutton Curry (Or Beef)	40
Irish Stew	41
Italian Braised Lamb And Potatoes	42
Japanese Lamb For Crockpot	43
Kadai Chop	44
Kakori Kabob	45
Korma – Lamb With Cashew-Nut Curry	46
Lamb and Apple Casserole	47
Lamb And Pine Nut Stir-Fry	48
Lamb Appetizer	49
Lamb Burgers With Sephardic Charoset	50
Lamb Chop With Jackfruit Gravy	50
Lamb Chops Creole	53
Lamb Chops with Moroccan Spices	54
Lamb Curry with Pumpkin	55
Lamb Shanks with Apricot Couscous	56
Lamb Shanks With Artichokes And Olives	57
Lamb Tagine with Artichokes and Mint	58
Lamb Tagine With Chickpeas And Raisins, Basmati Rice, Haris	59
Lamb Tagine with Potatoes and Chickpeas	61
Lamb Tandoori	63
Lamb With Arugula Dipping Sauce	64
Lamb With Butter Beans	64
Lamb With Honey And Cumin	66
Leg of Lamb with Garlic & Herbs	67
Light Stew	68
Liula-Kabob	69
Loubia	70
Marinated Lamb-and-Vegetable Kebabs	71
Maushawa (Pulse And Yoghurt Soup)	73
Moroccan Lamb Tagine with Raisins, Almonds, and Honey	74
Moroccan Spiced Meatballs W/ Eggs in Tomato Sauce	75
Moroccan-Style Meatballs	76
Moussaka (Lamb And Eggplant Casserole)	78

Chapter 2

N-Z **81**

Nargis Kofta – Boiled Eggs Wrapped In Spicy Meat –N. India	81
Pan-Broiled Lamb Chops	81
Pasanda Kabob	82
Pepper-Stuffed Lamb with Garlic Chevre Sauce	83

Table of Contents

Quick Cassoulet 84
Rack Of Lamb, Cranberry-Tangerine Sauce, Braised Red Chard 85
Racks of Lamb with White Beans 87
Really Simple Barbeque Sauce 88
Roast Lamb with Mint-Apple Couscous 89
Roast Leg of Lamb 91
Roast Leg of Lamb with Red Pepper Sabayon 92
Roast Leg Of Lamb With Small Onions 93
Roasted Tomato and Mint Salsa 95
Romanian Jewish Beef Sausages 96
Rosemary-Roasted Leg of Lamb with Balsamic Sauce 97
Royal Lamb Chops Braised With Nuts and Saffron 98
Safed Gosht - Lamb Stewed In Coconut Milk 99
Samoosa (Small Savory Pastries) 100
Sealed Pot Curry (Sindhi) 102
Seared Ahi Tuna With Eggplant Marmalade And Horseradish Cream 104
Sheftalia (Barbeque Sausages) 105
Shorba Of Vegetables 106
Slavonija Braised Lamb 107
Slow-Cooker Braised Lamb Shanks 108
Tandoori Leg of Lamb with Cucumber Raita 109
Tekkady Attarachi (Lamb Chops) 111
Turkari Palaak Molee 113
Yankee Lamb Stew 114

Index 116

Preface

Notice of Rights

All rights reserved. No part of this book may be reproduced or transmitted in any form by any means, electronic, mechanical, photocopying, recording, or otherwise, without the prior written permission of the publisher.

Notice of Liability

The information in this book is distributed on an "As Is" basis without warranty. While every precaution has been taken in the preparation of the book, neither the author nor the publisher shall have any liability to any person or entity with respect to any loss or damage caused or alleged to be caused directly or indirectly by the instructions contained in this book or by the products described in it.

Trademarks

Many of the designations used by manufacturers and sellers to distinguish their products are claimed as trademarks. Where those designations appear in this book, and the publisher was aware of a trademark claim, the designations appear as requested by the owner of the trademark. All other product names and services identified throughout this book are used in editorial fashion only and for the benefit of such companies with no intention of infringement of the trademark. No such use, or the use of any trade name, is intended to convey endorsement or other affiliation with this book.

Jo Franks

Chapter 1
A–M

ALGERIAN LAMB SHANKS WITH CARDAMOM AND ORANGE

4 servings
Source: Lamb Greats

- 4 lamb shanks, external fat trimmed
- Salt, to taste, plus 1 Tbs. salt
- Freshly ground pepper, to taste
- 4 tablespoons extra-virgin olive oil, plus more for serving
- 1 lb. yellow onions, diced
- ¼ cup peeled garlic cloves
- 1 tablespoon finely chopped fresh ginger
- 2 cardamom seeds, skins removed
- pn of saffron
- 1 teaspoon chili flakes
- 1 teaspoon ground cloves
- 1 teaspoon caraway seeds
- 2 teaspoons fennel seeds
- ½ cinnamon stick
- 2 tablespoons curry powder
- ½ cup blanched slivered almonds
- ½ cup golden raisins
- 2 cans (10 oz. each) diced plum tomatoes
- 1 bottle white wine
- Zest and juice of 1 orange
- 1 lb. carrots, peeled and coarsely diced
- 1 large fennel bulb, trimmed and coarsely diced

Preheat an oven to 350°F.

Generously season the lamb shanks with salt and pepper. In an ovenproof deep saute pan or Dutch oven over high heat, warm 2 Tbs. of the olive oil until nearly smoking. Working in batches, brown the shanks, 4 to 5 minutes per side. Transfer to a platter.

Add the remaining 2 Tbs. olive oil, the onions and garlic to the pan and saute, stirring, until the onions are tender and translucent, 4 to 5 minutes. Add the ginger, cardamom, saffron, chili flakes, cloves, caraway, fennel seeds, cinnamon, curry, the 1 Tbs. salt, almonds and raisins. Saute, stirring occasionally, about 5 minutes more. Add the tomatoes, wine, orange zest and orange juice and stir to mix well. Submerge the shanks in the liquid and bring to a simmer. Cover, transfer the pan to the oven and cook until the meat nearly falls off the bone, about 2 hours.

Stir the carrots and fennel bulb into the stew, cover and bake until the vegetables are tender, about 15 minutes more. Drizzle each serving with olive oil.

Comments: This braised lamb stew is wonderful served over a bed of steamed couscous. The couscous can be served plain or tossed with raisins, almonds and spices. Either way, it will absorb the flavorful broth from the stew.

ARNI LEMONATO (ROAST LEMON LAMB)

8 servings
Source: Lamb Greats

freshly ground black pepper

1 leg of lamb, about 2 kg (5 lbs.)

1 teaspoon **dried rigani or oregano**

3 **garlic cloves**

2 tablespoons **butter or margarine**

2 **lemons, (juice only)**

1 cup **hot water**

salt

Chapter 1: A–M

Preheat oven to 350°F

Wipe leg with damp cloth. Cut small slits over surface of lamb. Cut garlic cloves into slivers and insert in slits. Rub entire surface with lemon juice and season with salt and pepper. Sprinkle with herb and place in a roasting pan. Cook in a moderate oven for 1 hour. Drain off fat and add hot water to pan. Spread butter on lamb and return to oven. Cook for further 1 1/2 hours or until lamb is cooked to taste. Turn during cooking to brown evenly. Allow lamb to rest in warm place for 15 to 20 minutes before carving. Skim off excess fat from pan juices, reduce if necessary and serve with the lamb.

Note: 1 kg (2 lb.) potatoes, peeled and quartered, be cooked with the lamb during the last hour. Sprinkle with additional lemon juice, herb, salt and pepper.

ASIAN CREPINETTES

8 servings
Source: Lamb Greats

- 1 lb. **Ground Lamb**
- 4 tablespoons **Fresh Asian or reg.**
- **Basil (finely chopped)**
- 3 tablespoons **Minced Fresh Coriander**
- 1 tablespoon **Finely chopped Ginger**
- 2 teaspoons **Finely chopped Garlic**
- 1 teaspoon **Salt**
- 2 teaspoons **Sichuan Peppercorns roasted**
- **and ground**
- 2 teaspoons **Coarse. chopped dried chiles**
- 1 tablespoon **Light soy sauce**
- 1 tablespoon **Dark soy sauce**
- 2 tablespoons **Rice wine or dry sherry**
- 2 teaspoons **Chinese sesame oil**
- ½ lb. **Caul fat or crepinette**

Lamb Greats

Soak The Caul Fat in a bowl of cold water; this will allow the caul fat to unravel easily. In a medium-sized bowl, mix the ground lamb with all the ingredients except the caul fat. Cut the caul fat into (5-inch) squares.

Lay out a square of caul fat and place several tablespoons of lamb mixture onto one end. Fold the sides in to form a package. Repeat until you have used up all the lamb. Recipe can be done ahead to this point and refrigerated.

Wrap the crepinettes (caul fat) well in plastic wrap and refrigerate. Approximately 40 minutes before you are ready to cook, make a charcoal fire and, when the coals are ash white, grill the crepinettes (caul fat) for about 8 minutes on each side, or until they are done (firm to the touch).

Makes 6 to 8 Servings

BASIC KIBBI

1 servings
Source: Lamb Greats

2 ⅔ cups **bulgur, * see note**	⅛ teaspoon **cinnamon**
1 large onion, grated	⅛ teaspoon **allspice**
2 tablespoons **salt**	2 lbs. **ground lamb or beef**
¼ teaspoon **pepper**	

* Add an additional 1/2 cup when using lamb.

Cover bulgur with cold water, soak for 10 minutes. Drain and press between palms of hand to remove excess water. Work onions and spices together with fingers. Knead meat and spices together thoroughly; add crushed wheat and continue kneading.

Dip hands in ice water while kneading in order to soften kibbi. (Ingredients must be kept cold.) Run the kneaded mixture through a meat grinder one to three times for a finer consistency.

Note: When using beef, 1 1/4 teaspoon of ground sweet basil may be added.

BEEF OR LAMB BAKED WITH YOGURT AND BLACK PEPPER

1 servings
Source: Lamb Greats

- 6 tablespoons **oil**
- 2 lbs. **boneless stewing beef or lamb, cut in 1 1/2in cubes**
- 2 ½ large **onions, finely chopped**
- 6 cloves **garlic, minced**
- ½ teaspoon **ginger root**
- ¼ teaspoon **cayenne pepper, (to taste)**
- 1 tablespoon **paprika**
- 2 teaspoons **salt**
- ½ teaspoon **freshly ground black pepper**
- ½ pint **plain yogurt, lightly beaten**

Heat oil in casserole dish over med-high heat. Brown meat in single layer in batches. Remove browned meat to bowl.

Reduce heat to med. Add onions and garlic and fry 10mins. Return meat to casserole. Add remaining ingredients except yogurt. Stir 1 min. add yogurt and bring to a simmer.

Cover with aluminum foil and then with casserole lid. Bake in preheated 350°F oven 1 1/2 hours. Meat should be tender. If not add 1/2 cup water and bake another 25 mins.

Great with rice or naan.

Serves 4-6

BHARWAAN DUM KI RAAN

6 servings
Source: Lamb Greats

1 ½ kg **leg of lamb--slit along the length**, (3 1/2 pounds)

THE MARINADE

2 teaspoons **salt**

4 teaspoons **raw papaya paste**

4 teaspoons **ginger paste**

2 teaspoons **garlic paste**

¼ cup **red wine, (or malt vinegar)**

½ lb. **chicken breast, minced**

1 ¾ ounces **cheddar or processed cheese, grated**

2 ½ ounces **cream**

12 **pistachios, blanched and halved**

1 small **red bell pepper, chopped**

1 **green chile**

½ teaspoon **black pepper powder**

salt to taste

1 tablespoon **mint leaves, chopped**

1 sprig **rosemary (optional), chopped**

TO BRAISE

1 teaspoon **chile powder**

oil to baste the leg

3 **cardamom**

3 **cloves**

1 **black cardamom**

1 stick **cinnamon**

1 **star anise**

6 **rose petals**

THE GRAVY

75 g **ghee**

3 **cardamom**

2 **black cardamom**

1 **clove**

1 inch **cinnamon stick**

1 **bay leaf**

3 teaspoons **ginger paste**

2 teaspoons **garlic paste**

cashew nut paste

1 **clear lamb stock**

½ teaspoon **chile powder**

Chapter 1: A–M

½ cup **curd, beaten (120 ml)**

3 **onions, sliced, fried till crisp and crumbled**

5 **mint leaves, chopped**

3 g **coriander leaves, chopped**

salt to taste

¼ teaspoon **patthar ka phool powder**

1 g **rose petal powder**

a few strands saffron, dissolved in a little lukewarm water

FORCEFULLY rub, as in massage, the lamb leg, inside and out, with salt. Repeat the process with raw papaya paste, ginger paste and garlic paste and finally with vinegar. (Each of these ingredients should be rubbed separately and not as a mixture.) Reserve for one-and-a-half hours.

Put the chicken mince in a food processor or blender, add cheese, pulse for a few seconds. Add cream in a steady stream and pulse with little bursts until a fine mousse is obtained. Remove to a bowl, add the remaining ingredients and mix well.

Pry open the pockets and stuff the filling into the leg. Using the trussing needle and string, stitch the open ends. Bind the stuffed leg with string to retain the shape whilst cooking. Baste with butter and prick with a needle.

Forcefully rub, as in massage, the lamb leg with the red chiles, followed by oil. Arrange the leg in a roasting tray, add the remaining ingredients and enough water to cover the leg. Braise in a pre-heated oven (275°F) for two hours. Remove and discard the liqueur. Rub again with oil and keep aside.

Roast each of the ingredients for the cashew nut paste separately on a medium hot tawa, and grind to a smooth paste adding about 1 1/4 cups water.

Heat ghee in a large flat pan. Season with cardamom, black cardamom, cloves, cinnamon and bay leaf. Stir over medium heat until the green cardamom changes color. Add ginger paste and garlic paste, stir over medium heat until the moisture evaporates. Lower the heat, add cashew nut paste and stir-fry until the ghee floats on top (sprinkling small quantities of stock to prevent sticking). Add chile powder. Stir for a few seconds, remove the pan from heat, stir in the curd and return the pan to heat. Add fried onions and stir-fry until the ghee floats on top. Add the braised raan, and the remaining stock, bring to a boil, lower the heat and simmer for 45 minutes.

Remove the leg and snip off the strings. Pass the gravy through a fine mesh sieve into a separate saucepan. Return the gravy to heat, add the leg, mint leaves, coriander leaves and salt. Bring it to a boil, lower the heat, add patthar ke phool powder, rose petal powder and saffron. Simmer until the gravy is of ketchup consistency. Remove and adjust the seasoning.

To serve: Arrange the leg on a serving dish, pour the gravy over and serve hot.

BHUNAWA SALAN

1 servings
Source: Lamb Greats

2 ½ lbs. **lamb**

salt according to taste

¼ teaspoon **haldi powder (turmeric)**

1 teaspoon **chili powder**

1 tablespoon **dhuniya powder (coriander)**

1 medium **onion chopped**

3 tablespoons **oil, up to 4**

1 teaspoon **ginger paste**

½ teaspoon **garlic paste**

1 **tomato chopped**

6 whole **black pepper, up to 8**

3 **laung, (cloves), up to 4**

2 **bari illaichi**

¼ teaspoon **zeera**

Chapter 1: A–M

Fry the onion in the oil until brown. Mix all the ingredients together and add to the pot and stir til the tomato has become soft and the water has dried. Then add the meat and again let the water dry.

Add 3-4 glasses of water, cover and leave to tenderize.

When meat is almost done add any of the following vegetables: Palak, tomato, Cauliflower, Turnip (Shaljam), Beet, Zucchini.

Garnish with fresh dhuniya (cilantro) leaves and chopped green chiles.

BICHAK (STUFFED BAKED TRICORNERS)

1 servings
Source: Lamb Greats

DOUGH

1 ½ cups **water, warm**

1 teaspoon **sugar**

1 package **dry yeast**

3 ½ cups **flour**

3 tablespoons **corn oil**

1 **egg, separated**

1 **egg yolk, beaten with**

½ teaspoon **corn oil**

STUFFINGS

***SQUASH,

CALABASA, OR PUMPKIN***

¼ cup **corn oil**

2 medium **onions, chopped**

1 cup - **water, hot and 1/4 t salt**

2 tablespoons **sugar**

1 lb. **butternut squash, calabasa, or pumpkin,**

MEAT

2 tablespoons **corn oil**

3 medium (2 cups) **onion, chopped**

1 lb. **ground beef or lamb**

½ teaspoon **salt, or to taste**

¼ teaspoon **pepper, peeled and cut into 1/2-in pieces**

CHEESE

1 lb. **farmer cheese**

1 **egg yolk, beaten**

3 tablespoons **sugar**

½ teaspoon **ground cinnamon**

JAM

9

Lamb Greats

1 cup strawberry or grape or prune jam, (lekach)

2 tablespoons bread crumbs

Heat oil in a pan, add onions, and sauté over moderate heat until onions turn golden.

Add water, salt, sugar, and squash or calabasa or pumpkin and bring to a boil.

Cover pan and cook over low heat for about 20 minutes as squash/calabasa/pumpkin becomes soft and disintegrates.

Stir now and then, which in effect mashes contents.

Continue last minutes of cooking, uncovered, to evaporate all liquid and create and thick jam.

The mash is still moist.

MEAT:

Heat oil in a skillet and brown onions lightly over moderate heat.

Add meat, salt, and pepper and stir-fry for 5 minutes, making certain liquid has evaporated and mixture is dry. Cool.

CHEESE:

Mix everything together. Set aside.

JAM:

Mix jam and crumbs together. Set aside.

TO PREPARE TRICORNERS:

Chapter 1: A-M

Mix 1/2 c warm water, sugar, and yeast together and proof in a warm place until mixture foams, about 10 minutes.

Make a well in flour, add yeast mixture, oil, and 1 egg white, and stir them into flour.

Add balance of water, or enough water to prepare a soft dough.

Knead for several minutes and roll into a ball. Oil top lightly and leave dough in mixing bowl.

Cover bowl w/foil or a towel and let rise for 45 minutes to 1 hour.

Punch down dough ball. Pull off about 1/2 cup of dough and roll into a slightly flattened ball. Prepare 6 balls.

On well-floured board roll out each ball, 1 at a time, to 12-" pancake. Using empty can or a cookie cutter, 3-" in diameter, cut out circles in pancake.

Put 1 tb of whichever stuffing you are using, or variety of stuffings, in center of each circle.

Fold over right and left side of circle to meet in the center and bring up bottom to cover stuffing.

Pinch ends together to form tricorner pastry. Seal in contents. Paint tops of bichak w/egg yolk.

Line baking pan or cookie sheet w/lightly oiled aluminum foil.

Place tricorners on foil and bake in a preheated 350°F. oven for about 40 minutes, or until brown. Serve warm.

Note:

Cool bichak, store in plastic bags, and freeze.

Lamb Greats

To serve, thaw out frozen bichak for 1/2 hour and heat in preheated 350°F. oven for 5-10 minutes.

BRAISED LAMB SHANKS WITH ROASTED POTATOES

6 servings
Source: Lamb Greats

- 6 **lamb shanks, well trimmed**
- **Salt and freshly ground pepper, to taste**
- ¼ cup **vegetable oil, plus more as needed**
- 2 **yellow onions, diced**
- 2 **celery stalks, diced**
- 2 **carrots, peeled and diced**
- 4 **large garlic cloves, minced**
- 1 cup **full-bodied red wine**
- 2 cups **diced canned tomatoes, drained**
- 2 ½ cups **beef stock**
- 2 teaspoons **minced fresh rosemary**
- 1 teaspoon **minced fresh thyme**
- 2 **bay leaves**
- 2 lbs. **baby new potatoes**
- 3 tablespoons **extra-virgin olive oil**
- 1 teaspoon **salt**
- ½ teaspoon **freshly ground pepper**
- 1 tablespoon **red wine vinegar**
- **Minced fresh flat-leaf parsley for garnish**
- 3 tablespoons **Olivier Parmesan dipping and drizzling oil**

Preheat an oven to 400°F.

Generously season the lamb shanks with salt and pepper. In a large oval Dutch oven over medium-high heat, warm the 1/4 cup vegetable oil. Working in batches, brown the shanks on all sides, 5 to 10 minutes total, adding more oil to the pan if needed. Transfer to a platter. Pour off the excess fat from the pan.

Add the onions, celery and carrots to the pan and cook, stirring occasionally, until the vegetables are golden and translucent, 5 to 8 minutes. Add the garlic and saute for 2 minutes. Remove the pan from the heat and add the wine. Return the pan to medium-high heat and bring the liquid to a simmer, stirring to scrape up the browned bits.

Simmer until the liquid is reduced by half, about 5 minutes. Add the tomatoes, stock, rosemary, thyme, bay leaves and lamb shanks and bring to a boil. Cover the pan, transfer to the oven and cook until the meat is almost falling off the bone, 1 1/2 to 2 hours. Using tongs, transfer the shanks to a large serving bowl and cover loosely with aluminum foil.

Increase the oven temperature to 450°F. Oil a baking sheet or roasting pan. In a large bowl, stir together the potatoes, olive oil, 1 tsp. salt and 1/2 tsp. pepper. Arrange the potatoes on the prepared pan. Roast, stirring and turning the potatoes occasionally, until tender when pierced with a fork, 30 to 35 minutes.

Meanwhile, remove the bay leaves from the cooking liquid and discard. Skim off the fat. Using an immersion blender, puree until smooth. Stir in the vinegar and season with salt and pepper. Pour some of the sauce over the shanks and garnish with parsley. Transfer the remaining sauce to a sauce boat.

Transfer the potatoes to a cutting board and cut in half. Place in a large bowl, add the Parmesan oil and stir to coat. Transfer to a serving bowl and garnish with parsley. Serve the lamb shanks and pass the potatoes and the sauce alongside.

Comments: These lamb shanks are slow-cooked until the meat is almost falling off the bone. They're delicious paired with roasted baby potatoes, which get a flavor boost from Parmesan-infused olive oil.

BRAISED LAMB SHANKS WITH WHITE BEANS

6 servings
Source: Lamb Greats

- 1 ½ cups **dried small white, white kidney or cannellini beans**
- 2 tablespoons **extra-virgin olive oil**
- 6 **lamb shanks, each 1/2 to 3/4 lb.**
- 1 **yellow onion, finely diced**
- 1 **celery stalk, finely diced**
- 2 **large carrots, peeled and finely diced**
- 6 **garlic cloves, minced**
- 1 ½ cups **dry red wine such Cabernet Sauvignon or Chianti**
- 1 ½ cups **chicken broth**
- 1 ½ cups **peeled, seeded and chopped tomatoes (fresh or canned)**
- 3 tablespoons **tomato paste**
- 1 teaspoon **chopped fresh thyme**
- 1 **bay leaf**
- **Salt and freshly ground pepper, to taste**
- 1 tablespoon **shredded lemon zest**
- 2 tablespoons **chopped fresh flat-leaf parsley**

Pick over the beans and discard any misshapen beans and stones. Rinse the beans, place in a bowl and add water to cover generously. Let stand for about 3 hours.

Drain the beans and place in a saucepan with water to cover by 2 inches. Place over medium-high heat and bring to a boil. Reduce the heat to low and simmer, uncovered, until nearly tender, 45 to 60 minutes. Drain well.

Meanwhile, in a deep, heavy stock pot over medium heat, warm the olive oil. Add the lamb shanks and brown on all sides, 10 to 12 minutes. Transfer the shanks to a plate. Add the onion, celery and carrots to the pan and saute over medium heat, stirring occasionally, until the onion is soft, about 10 minutes. Add the garlic and cook, stirring, for 1 minute. Add the wine, broth, tomatoes, tomato paste, thyme, bay leaf and lamb shanks. Bring to a boil over high heat. Reduce the heat to low, cover and simmer until the shanks can be easily pierced with a skewer, 1 1/2 to 2 hours.

Add the beans, stir well, cover and simmer gently until the lamb begins to fall from the bone and the beans are tender, about 30 minutes more. Season with salt and pepper. Remove the bay leaf and discard.

In a small bowl, stir together the lemon zest and parsley. Transfer the lamb shanks and beans to individual plates and garnish with the lemon zest-parsley mixture. Serve immediately.

Comments: Lamb shanks, white beans, tomatoes and red wine are an ideal union for a hearty autumn dinner. You can substitute the same amount of veal shanks for the lamb shanks if you like.

BRAISED LAMB SHOULDER WITH FIGS

6 servings
Source: Lamb Greats

1 boneless lamb shoulder, 4 to 4 1/2 lb., rolled and tied, bones cut into pieces

Salt and freshly ground pepper, to taste

All-purpose flour for dredging

4 to 5 t olive oil

1 large yellow onion, thinly sliced

4 large garlic cloves, crushed with the side of a knife

½-inch-wide strips of peel from 1 lemon (with no bitter white pith)

1 cup **dry red wine**

1 cup **chicken stock**

1 tablespoon **tomato paste**

1 teaspoon **dried oregano**

¼ teaspoon **ground cinnamon**

Lamb Greats

⅛ teaspoon **ground cloves**

6 **large dried figs, about 8 oz. total, hard stems**

trimmed, figs halved or quartered

1 tablespoon **chopped fresh dill**

Preheat an oven to 325°F.

Pat the lamb dry with paper towels and season with salt and pepper. Put the flour in a shallow bowl and dredge the lamb in the flour, shaking off the excess.

In a large heavy pot over medium-high heat, warm 4 tsp. of the olive oil. Add the meat and bones and brown on all sides, about 10 minutes. Transfer them to a platter. Reduce the heat to low and add the onion, garlic and lemon peel to the pan along with the remaining 1 tsp. oil, if needed. Cook, stirring frequently to incorporate some of the browned bits, until the onion starts to wilt, about 3 minutes.

Lay the meat and bones on the onion mixture and add the wine, stock and tomato paste. Bring to a simmer and add the oregano, cinnamon and cloves. Cover the pot and transfer to the oven. Cook until the meat is very tender, about 2 1/4 hours, adding the figs during the last 30 minutes of cooking.

Transfer the meat and figs to a platter, cover loosely with aluminum foil and let rest for 15 to 20 minutes. Discard the bones and skim the fat from the sauce. Set the pot over low heat and simmer until the sauce is slightly thickened, flavorful and reduced to about 1 1/4 cups, about 10 minutes. Taste and adjust the seasonings with salt and pepper.

Discard the strings from the lamb, slice the meat across the grain and arrange the slices on the platter, surrounded by the figs. Spoon some of the sauce over the meat and sprinkle with the dill. Transfer the remaining sauce to a sauceboat and pass alongside.

Comments: Ask the butcher to give you the lamb bones so you can add them to the pot. They will contribute flavor to the subtly fig-sweetened sauce. If you'd like, garnish the finished dish with halved fresh figs.

BROILED LAMB CHOPS WITH BRAISED ROOT VEGETABLES, COLCANNON

4 servings
Source: Lamb Greats

=== **BRAISED ROOT VEGETABLES** ===

2 tablespoons **butter**

1 lb. **packaged baby carrots**

1 **rutabaga, peeled, diced**

1 **onion, diced**

Salt, to taste

Freshly-ground black pepper, to taste

2 cups **chicken or vegetable stock**

=== **LAMB** ===

8 **loin lamb chops**

Salt, to taste

Freshly-ground black pepper, to taste

=== **COLCANNON** ===

4 medium to large **all-purpose potatoes, peeled, and cut into chunks**

Coarse salt, for boiling water

2 cups **chicken or vegetable stock**

1 head **dark curly kale, chopped**

2 tablespoons **butter**

¾ cup **whole milk**

¼ teaspoon **fresh or grated nutmeg**

1 teaspoon **ground thyme**

2 **scallions, sliced**

A handful of **fresh parsley, chopped**

=== **ACCOMPANIMENTS** ===

Prepared store-bought Irish soda bread or

brown bread, warmed, for passing

at table

Softened sweet butter, for the bread

For braised vegetables: Heat a skillet with a cover over medium to medium-high heat. Add butter, carrots, rutabaga and onion. Cook veggies 5 minutes, stirring frequently. Add broth or stock, bring to a simmer, and reduce heat and cover. Cook vegetables 15 minutes or until fork tender. Remove from heat and set aside.

Preheat broiler to high for lamb.

Boil potatoes for 15 minutes in salted water. Drain potatoes and return them to the hot pot and mash.

Heat stock or broth to a simmer. Chop kale tops, discarding tough stems. Add kale to broth and cover. Simmer 10 to 12 minutes.

Place chops about 6 to 8 inches from broiler and cook 5 minutes on each side. Remove from broiler and season chops with salt and pepper on both sides. Let chops rest 3 to 5 minutes.

In a large skillet over moderate heat melt butter and add milk. Season with nutmeg and thyme and add scallions to the pan. Remove kale from cooking liquid to the milk and butter mixture using a slotted spoon. Stir in 1/2 cup of cooking liquid. Add mashed potatoes to milk and kale and stir until combined and creamy, 1 or 2 minutes. Stir in parsley and season with salt and pepper, to taste.

Serve the chops along with vegetable colcannon. Warm up store-bought Irish soda bread or brown bread with soft, unsweetened butter. This makes a nice starter, side or ending to this meal.

This recipe yields 4 servings.

BURGOO

1 servings
Source: Lamb Greats

3 qt **water or stock**

- ¾ lbs. **lean inch-diced stewing beef**
- ¾ lbs. **inch-diced pork shoulder**
- 3 ½ lbs. **chicken, disjointed**
- **water to cover**
- 2 ½ cups **ripe tomatoes, quartered, peeled and seeded**
- 1 cup **fresh lima beans**
- ½ **red pepper, diced**
- 4 **green peppers, diced**
- ¾ cups **onion, diced**
- 1 cup **carrots, diced**
- 2 cups **potatoes, diced**
- 1 **bay leaf**
- 1 tablespoon **Worcestershire sauce**
- 2 cups **corn freshly cut from the cob**

Mulligan stew is said to have originated in hobo camps during the early 1900s, mulligan stew is a sort of catch-all dish of whatever is available. It usually contains meat, potatoes and vegetables in just about any combination. The name indicates that its origins might come from IRISH STEW, but it's also often compared to Kentucky BURGOO. The cook at a hobo camp responsible for putting this tasty concoction together was called a "mulligan-mixer."

If you are like most people you have never heard of much less eaten burgoo. This is one of those times its definitely best to be in the minority. Burgoo is a savory stew made from a varying array of ingredients. If is often cooked in enormous iron kettles outdoors over an open flame. Cooking can take as long as 30 hours and flavor improves as it ages. It has been said that burgoo is more of a concept than a recipe.

This is because there are as many different ways to prepare burgoo as there are people who prepare it. The meats could include any or all of the following meats: mutton (sheep/lamb), beef, pork, chicken, veal or opossum, rabbit, squirrel You will also find some combination of these vegetables: potatoes, corn, lima beans, tomatoes, okra or green beans. Of course there are also many spices to choose from as well. As you might imagine there are many people who keep their recipes a closely guarded secret.

Lamb Greats

Put in a heavy lidded kettle with:

qts. water or stock 1/4 lb. lean inch-diced stewing beef 1/4 lb. inch-diced pork shoulder

Bring pot one slowly to a boil. Reduce heat at once and slowly simmer about 2 1/2 hours.

In another heavy kettle put:

One disjointed 3 1/2 lb. chicken with just enough water to cover. Bring these ingredients to a boil. Reduce the heat at once and simmer about 1 hour or until the meat can easily be removed from the bones. Put the chicken meat and the water in which it was cooked into the first kettle with the other meat after it has simmered the 2 1/2 hours as directed.

At this time also add:

1/2 cups quartered ripe, peeled and seeded tomatoes cup fresh lima beans 1/2 red diced pepper diced green peppers 1/4 cup diced onion cup diced carrots cups diced potatoes bay leaf Tablespoon Worcestershire sauce

Simmer this whole mixture 1/2 hour or more before adding

1 cups corn (freshly cut from cob) Cook about 15 minutes more or until all the vegetables are soft. Correct the seasoning.

BUTTERFLIED LEG OF LAMB

8 servings
Source: Lamb Greats

1 leg of lamb, 5 to 6 lb., trimmed of fat, boned and butterflied

7 large garlic cloves

Coarse salt and freshly

Chapter 1: A–M

ground pepper, to taste
1 bottle full-bodied red wine
9 oil-packed
sun-dried tomatoes, drained
½ cup **pitted oil-cured olives, plus extra for garnish**

2 tablespoons **herbes de Provence**
2 teaspoons **freshly ground pepper**
1 to 2 t **olive oil, or as needed**
Chopped fresh flat-leaf parsley

Make 15 to 20 small slits at regular intervals in the butterflied lamb. Sliver 2 of the garlic cloves and insert into the slits. Season the meat with salt and pepper. Place the lamb in a large lock-top plastic bag or a nonaluminum dish and add 2 cups of the wine. Seal the bag securely or cover the dish. Refrigerate for at least 3 hours or for up to 3 days, turning occasionally. Bring the lamb to room temperature before roasting.

On a cutting board, place the remaining 5 garlic cloves, sprinkle with a few pinches of coarse salt, then chop. Add the sun-dried tomatoes,

1/2 cup olives, herbes de Provence and the 2 tsp. pepper and continue to chop to form a coarse paste.

Preheat an oven to 450°F. Remove the lamb from the marinade and lay it flat, cut side up. Pour the marinade into a small saucepan, bring to a boil and remove from the heat. Evenly spread the tomato-olive paste over the meat. Roll up the lamb and tie securely with kitchen string at intervals of 2 to 3 inches.

In a roasting pan over high heat, warm enough olive oil to form a film on the pan bottom. Add the lamb and brown on all sides, 5 to 6 minutes total. Transfer to the oven and roast for 15 minutes. Reduce the oven temperature to 350∞F and continue to roast, basting every 10 to 15 minutes with the reserved marinade, until an instant-read thermometer inserted into the thickest part of the meat registers 125°F to 130°F for very rare to medium-rare, about 45 minutes.

Alternatively, cut into the meat with a sharp knife; it should be pink or done to your liking. Transfer to a cutting board, cover loosely with aluminum foil and let rest for 10 minutes before carving.

Meanwhile, place the roasting pan over high heat. Add 1 cup of the wine and deglaze the pan, stirring to scrape up any browned bits from the pan bottom. Bring to a boil and boil until reduced by half, 5 to 8 minutes. Spoon off the fat from the pan juices, then strain through a fine-mesh sieve into a warmed sauceboat.

Snip the strings and carve the lamb across the grain into thin slices. Arrange on a warmed platter, sprinkle with chopped parsley and garnish with the olives. Pass the pan juices at the table.

CARNERO EN ADOBE – TANGY BRAISED LAMB SHANKS

4 servings
Source: Lamb Greats

2 **Ancho chilies**

1 cup **Boiling water**

2 tablespoons **Vegetable oil**

4 **Lamb shanks**

2 md **White onions, halved**

⅓ cup **Raisins**

2 tablespoons **Piloncillo, Mexican hard sauce**

4 cups **Garlic, minced**

⅜ teaspoons **Oregano**

½ teaspoon **Cumin**

28 ounces **Tomato, whole peeled**

¾ cups **Beef stock**

4 **Bay leaf**

1 tablespoon **Cider vinegar**

Romaine lettuce, shredded

Black olives, pitted

Place chilies in small bowl with boiling water, let stand 1 hour.

Heat lard or oil in Dutch oven over med. heat until hot. Add 2 lamb shanks. Cook turning often, until brown on all sides about 20 minutes. Remove to plate. Repeat.

Place chilies and 1/3 cup of the soaking liquid in a blender and process until smooth. Discard remaining soaking liquid.

Remove and discard all but 2 TBS oil from Dutch oven. Add onions and saute' over medium heat about 4 mins. or until soft. Reduce heat to med-low and stir in raisins, sugar, garlic, oregano and cumin. Add chili puree and cook stirring constantly for 2 minutes.

Add tomatoes, stock and bay leaves to pan. Heat to boiling. Add lamb shanks and simmer over low heat, covered, turning occasionally until lamb is very, very tender--about to 2/12 hours

Remove lamb to serving platter and keep warm. Skim and discard fat from cooking sauce. Stir in vinegar. Heat sauce to boiling over med.-high heat and cook uncovered, stirring frequently until sauce is thickened--about 10 minutes. Spoon sauce over lamb. Serve, garnished with lettuce and olives (be even some quartered tomatoes).

Accompany with Refried Beans garnished as desired with shredded cheese and diced white onions. I recommend with shanks that you clean them as well as possible of as much fat as possible plus that white membrane. don't remove all the membrane, however, as something has to hold them together.

CHAPPAL KEBAB - HAMBURGER KEBABS

4 servings
Source: Lamb Greats

1 tablespoon **chickpea flour, called gram flour or besan**

1 ½ lbs. **ground beef or lamb, ground quite fine**

½ cup **fresh cilantro leaves, coarsely chopped**

2 fresh hot green chilies **cut in rounds, with seeds**

1 ½ teaspoons **cumin seeds**

1 ½ teaspoons **coriander seeds**

Lamb Greats

1 teaspoon **freshly ground black pepper**
¼ teaspoon **salt**
½ **egg, lightly beaten**
¼ cup **vegetable oil**

Put chickpea flour in small cast-iron frying pan and stir around over medium heat until flour has turned a light brown color. Put it into bowl.

Add all other ingredients except oil and mix well. Form ten 2-inch balls. Fatten the balls to make 10 3 1/2-inch hamburger patties.

Just before eating put 2 tablespoons of oil into large nonstick frying pan and set over medium-high heat.

When oil is hot put in as many kebabs as the pan will hold in single layer. Turning them over every 20 seconds or so cook the kebabs for about 2 1/2 minutes or until they have browned on both sides.

Remove to warm plate. Use remaining oil to cook second batch.

CHICKEN OR LAMB BIRYANI

1 servings
Source: Lamb Greats

--**for the meat**---
2 ½ lbs. **lamb or chicken**
1 teaspoon **coriander powder**
½ teaspoon **ground cloves**
1 teaspoon **cumin powder**
¼ teaspoon **black pepper, ground**
1 teaspoon **chili powder, (cayenne)**
½ teaspoon **ground cinnamon**
½ teaspoon **cardamom powder**
½ pint **yogurt**
1 juice of on **lemon**
30 **garlic**
salt to taste
1 fresh **ginger**, (or 1 ts ground ginger)
4 large **onions**

Chapter 1: A-M

- 8 ounces **oil, (canola preferable)** -for the rice---
- 1 ½ lbs. **rice**
- 5 **bay leaves**
- 6 **green cardamoms, (may substitute black)**
- 10 whole **cloves**
- 4 small **cinnamon sticks**
- 10 **black peppercorns**
- 4 teaspoons **salt**
- ½ teaspoon **saffron strands**
- 2 teaspoons **milk**

Wash meat and cut into 1-inch cubes; place in bowl with ground spices, yogurt, lemon juice, finely chopped garlic and salt. If fresh ginger is used, chop finely and add to meat. Slice the onions finely and fry them in the oil until crisp and golden brown. Remove onions and put two-thirds into the meat mixture..

Soak the rice for one hour before cooking. Fill large pan 3/4 full with water. Put rice spices and salt into the water and bring to a boil. Add the rice and remove from heat after six minutes. Drain thoroughly without rinsing and spread onto a large flat dish to cool.

Mix saffron in hot milk. In a large pan, put in the meat and yogurt mixture and cover with the rice; pour in the spiced oil from the onions and the saffron/milk mixture.

Bring to a boil, then put in the oven for 1 hour or more. After 30 minutes, reduce heat. Stir before serving and sprinkle remaining fried onions top.

CHILI WITH LAMB AND BLACK BEANS

8 servings
Source: Lamb Greats

- 1 ¾ cups **Black beans, sorted rinsed**
- 2 qt **Water, or more as needed**
- 2 lbs. **Lamb bones**

Lamb Greats

- 4 **Thyme sprigs**
- 4 **Parsley sprigs**
- 1 **Bay leaf**
- 3 **Garlic clove, crushed**
- 6 tablespoons **Olive oil**
- 2 **Onions, lg yel, chopped**
- 1 ½ lbs. **Lamb shoulder, ground**
- 2 tablespoons **Chili powder**
- **Salt as needed**
- 2 tablespoons **Ginger, fresh minced**
- 2 tablespoons **Thyme, fresh minced or**
- 2 teaspoons **Thyme, dried crumbled**
- 1 tablespoon **Jalapeno, seeded, deveined**
- 1 ¼ teaspoons **Marjoram, dried, crumbled**
- ¾ teaspoons **White pepper, fresh ground**
- ¾ teaspoons **Black pepper, fresh ground**
- ¾ teaspoons **Pepper, cayenne**
- ¾ teaspoons **Allspice**
- 2 lbs. **Italian tomatoes, chopped**
- 1 ¼ cups **Wine, light zinfandel**

FOR BEANS: Soak Beans overnight in 2 qt. Water. In a large saucepan, bring Beans to a boil. Add lamb bones and bouquet garni and 1 crushed garlic clove.

Reduce heat and simmer till Beans are tender but not mushy. Skim occasionally and add more Water if necessary to keep Beans submerged. 2 hrs.

FOR CHILI: Heat 3 T. Oil in large heavy saucepan over moderate heat. Add Onions and cook until soft, about 10 minutes. Add 2 cloves garlic, minced, and stir about 3 minutes. Transfer Onion and garlic mixture to a plate, using a slotted spoon. Add remaining Oil to pan. Increase heat to med. high. Add lamb and cook until no longer pink, breaking up with spoon, about 6 min. Return Onion mixture to pan; add Chili powder, Ginger, thyme, red Chili, marjoram, Peppers and allspice. Stir 5 minutes.

Add Tomatoes (and half of their liquid, if canned). Bring to a boil then reduce heat and simmer for another 5 minutes. Add 3/4 c of

Chapter 1: A-M

Zinfandel.

Simmer, skimming occasionally, for 30 minutes. Drain Beans and reserve the cooking liquid. Discard the bones and garni. Add Beans and remaining Zinfandel to Chili mixture.

Salt and season as necessary. Simmer 30 minutes, adding bean cooking liquid as needed to keep Chili moist (or soupy, as you like it). This Chili is best made ahead and allowed to season in the refrigerator for 24 hours. Reheat before serving.

COCKTAIL KABOBS

1 servings
Source: Lamb Greats

50 g **boneless lamb**	11 g **split gram, (tuwar dal)**
1 **egg**	1 **bunch cilantro**
8 g **garam masala**	1 5 g **green chiles**
1 0 g **ginger**	6 0 g **onions, chopped**
oil for frying	**salt to taste**
4 **red chiles**	

Boil lamb, split gram, red chiles, 2 onions, ginger, salt in water. Remove water and grind to a fine paste. To this, add beaten egg, garam masala and mix well. Make equal small balls and keep aside.

In a separate bowl, add chopped onions, green chiles, coriander leaves, salt and mix well. Make into small balls.

Take one lamb ball, place in your palm, press to an oval shape. In this, place onion ball and close the edges.

Deep fry in oil until brown crispy kabobs.

DINGLE PIE

6 servings
Source: Lamb Greats

Stock:
Lamb bones from the meat
1 carrot
1 onion
Stalk celery
Bouquet garni (thyme sprig, parsley stalks and small bay leaf) tied with string
Filling:
1 lb. (450 grams) boneless lamb or mutton (from the shoulder or leg; keep bones for stock)
9 ounces (255 grams/ 2 1/4 cups) chopped onions
9 ounces (255 grams/ 1 3/4 cups) chopped carrots
2 good teaspoons cumin seed
2 American tablespoons, plus 2 teaspoons flour (2 Irish tablespoons) *see note

10 fluid ounces (300 milliliters/ 1 ¼ cups) mutton or lamb stock
Salt and freshly ground pepper
Pastry:
1 lb. (450 grams/3 1/2 cups) flour
pn salt
9 ounces (275 grams/2 1/4 cups) butter
6 fluid ounces (175 milliliters/3/4 cup) water
Egg Wash:
Water
1 egg, slightly beaten
pn salt
2 tins, 6 inches (15 cm) in diameter, 1 1/2 inches (4 centimeters) high

Preheat oven 400°F (200°C).

Stock: If no stock is available, put the bones, carrots, onions, celery and bouquet garni into a saucepan. Cover with cold water and simmer for 3 to 4 hours to make a stock. Strain and set aside.

Filling: Cut all the surplus fat away from the meat and then cut the meat into small, neat pieces about the size of a small sugar lump. Render down the scraps of fat in a hot, wide saucepan until the fat renders. Discard the pieces. Cut the vegetables into slightly smaller dice and toss them in the fat, leaving them to cook for 3 to 4 minutes. Remove the vegetables and toss the meat in the remaining fat over a high heat until the color turns deep brown.

Heat the cumin seed in the oven for a few minutes and crush lightly. Stir the flour and cumin seed into the meat. Cook gently for 2 minutes and add in the stock gradually. Bring to a boil, stirring occasionally. Add back the vegetables, season with salt and freshly ground pepper and leave to simmer, covered. If using young lamb, 30 minutes will be sufficient; an older animal may take up to 1 hour.

Pastry: Meanwhile, make the pastry. Sift the flour and salt into a mixing bowl and make a well in the center. Dice the butter, put it into a saucepan with water and bring to a boil. Pour the liquid all at once into the flour and mix together quickly; beat until smooth. At first the pastry will be too soft to handle but as soon as it cools it may be rolled out to 1/3 to 1/4- inch (2.5 to 5 millimeters) thick, to fit the 2 tins. The pastry may be made into individual pies or 1 large pie. Keep back 1/3 of the pastry for lids.

Fill the pastry-lined tins with the meat mixture which should be almost, but not quite cooked and cooled a little. Brush the edges of the pastry with the water and egg wash and put on the pastry lids, pinching them tightly together. Roll out the trimmings to make pastry leaves or twirls to decorate the tops of the pies. Make a hole in the center, brush the lid with egg-wash and then egg-wash the decoration also.

Bake the pies for 40 minutes. Serve with a good green salad.

Author Note: *Note: an Irish tablespoon is the same quantity as an American tablespoon plus a teaspoon.

DOLMADES (STUFFED GRAPE LEAVES)

1 servings
Source: Lamb Greats

- ½ **medium onion, minced**
- ¼ cup **uncooked rice, plus**
- 2 tablespoons **uncooked rice**
- 8 ounces **ground lamb**
- 8 ounces **ground beef**
- 1 clove **garlic, minced**
- 3 tablespoons **flat-leaf parsley, chopped**
- 1 **small carrot, peeled, diced fine**
- 1 teaspoon **grated lemon zest**
- 4 tablespoons **olive oil**
- 1 tablespoon **fresh mint, minced**
- 3 sprigs **fresh mint**
- ½ teaspoon **salt**
- ¼ teaspoon **freshly-ground black pepper**
- ½ jar **grape leaves – (16-oz jar), rinsed**
- 3 cups **chicken stock**
- 4 slices **lemon**

Heat oven to 325 degrees. In a bowl, combine onion, rice, lamb, beef, garlic, parsley, carrot, zest, 1 tablespoon oil, chopped mint, salt and pepper.

Place a leaf, vein side up, on a work surface; place about 1 tablespoon filling just below center. Fold bottom of leaf over filling and sides in toward center; roll up. Do not overfill or roll too tightly. Repeat, making 35.

Lay dolmades, seam-side down, in a 9- by 13-inch glass baking pan; do not pack tightly.

Combine stock and remaining 3 tablespoons oil; pour over dolmades. Squeeze lemon over dolmades, and place lemon slices and mint sprigs on top. Place another 9- by 13-inch baking pan, half full of water, on top to weigh down dolmades.

Bake for 40 to 50 minutes. Let dolmades cool in cooking liquid, still weighted, for 2 hours. Serve drizzled with olive oil, or refrigerate for up to 2 days; bring to room temperature before serving.

This recipe yields 35 dolmades.

EASY LAMB CREOLE GUMBO

8 servings
Source: Lamb Greats

2 tablespoons **vegetable oil**
½ **lemon, sliced/seeded**
flour
2 teaspoons **salt**
2 lbs. **lamb riblets**
1 teaspoon **thyme**
2 **cans stewed tomatoes, (16oz)**
1 **bay leaf**
4 cups **chicken broth**
1 teaspoon **instant minced garlic**
1 cup **white wine**
1 **package frozen sliced okra, (10oz)**
½ cup **chopped parsley**
1 **can black-eyed peas, (15oz)**

Heat oil in large Dutch oven; dust riblets with flour and brown on all sides in hot oil.

Drain fat from pan; add tomatoes, broth, wine, parsley, lemon slices and seasonings.

Cover and simmer 1 1/2 hours.

Add okra and peas; cook, covered, 10 to 15 minutes.

NOTE: Meat may be removed from bones before servings. This gumbo freezes well.

FETA AND BLACK OLIVE CRUSTED ROASTED LEG OF LAMB

8 servings
Source: Lamb Greats

- 5 lbs. **butterflied boned spring leg of lamb, fat and fell removed**
- 4 tablespoons **olive oil**
- 2 cloves **garlic**
- ½ teaspoon **minced garlic**
- 2 teaspoons **crushed red pepper flakes**
- **Zest of 1 orange**
- 1 tablespoon **fennel seeds**
- 1 ½ tablespoons **cardamom pods**
- 1 tablespoon **ground ginger**
- 2 tablespoons **unsalted butter**
- 1 cup **dry bread crumbs**
- 2 tablespoons **chopped fresh parsley**
- 1 cup **Olive Tapenade, (see below)**
- 1 cup **feta cheese (preferably Bulgarian), crumbled**
- 1 tablespoon **coarse salt**
- ½ teaspoon **freshly-cracked black pepper**
- 2 cups **small dandelion greens, for garnish**

=== OLIVE TAPENADE ===

- 1 tablespoon **olive oil**
- 3 cloves **garlic, roughly chopped**
- 5 whole **salt-packed anchovy fillets, rinsed**
- 2 tablespoons **capers**
- 1 ½ cups **Moroccan oil-cured olives**
- 1 teaspoon **finely-chopped fresh rosemary**
- **Freshly-ground black pepper, to taste**

Cover lamb with plastic wrap. Using a meat pounder, pound lamb to flatten slightly. Set aside.

Using a mortar and pestle or food processor, combine and coarsely grind 3 tablespoons olive oil, 2 cloves garlic, red pepper flakes, orange zest, fennel, cardamom, and ginger. Place lamb in a deep casserole or roasting pan. Add spice mixture, and turn to coat well. Cover, and refrigerate at least 2 hours, or up to 12 hours.

Remove lamb from refrigerator, and bring to room temperature. Heat broiler. Remove lamb from marinade, and place on a baking pan. Broil 3 to 4 inches from heat source, 5 minutes on each side.

In a saute pan, melt butter over medium-high heat. Add minced garlic, bread crumbs, and parsley. Cook until lightly browned. Season with salt and pepper. Remove from heat, and set aside.

To make the Olive Tapenade, in a saute pan over medium heat, add all ingredients and cook 3 to 4 minutes. Place mixture in food processor, and pulse until smooth. (Makes 1 3/4 cups).

Remove lamb from oven. Season with salt and pepper. Using a spatula, carefully spread an even layer of olive tapenade over lamb. Cover tapenade with feta cheese. Sprinkle with bread-crumb mixture and season with salt and pepper. Place lamb under broiler until browned, 8 to 10 minutes. Remove, and let rest 5 minutes before slicing.

Heat remaining 1 tablespoon olive oil in a large skillet over medium-high heat. Add dandelion greens and saute until just wilted, about 30 seconds. Transfer to platter, and top with sliced lamb.

This recipe yields 8 to 10 servings.

FRENCH ONION LAMB AU JUS

1 servings
Source: Lamb Greats

Lamb leg, rolled	1 package **Onion soup mix** (1.5 oz)
Garlic clove, minced	2 x **Onions, large sweet; sliced**
5 cups **Water**	
½ cup **Soy sauce**	

Combine all ingredients in a crock pot.

Cook 8 to 10 hours on low. Remove roast and let set 20 minutes before carving. Slice thin.

Make sandwiches using french rolls or large croissants, sliced and buttered with slices of Swiss Cheese.

Dip in bowls of the onion soup broth. Also can be made into a complete dinner by adding vegetables to the broth.

FRUIT-BRAISED LAMB SHANKS

5 servings
Source: Lamb Greats

- 1 tablespoon **butter**
- 1 tablespoon **vegetable oil**
- 2 **lamb shanks, about 1 1/2 to 2 pounds**
- ½ **onion, minced**
- 1 **clove garlic, minced**
- 1 **fresh or 1/2 dry bay leaf**
- 1 teaspoon **fresh thyme leaves**
- 1 tablespoon **flour**
- 1 tablespoon **turmeric**
- ½ teaspoon **dried chili flakes**
- ¾ cups **dry white wine, such as Chardonay or Sauvignon Blanc**
- 2 cups **chicken broth**
- 2 **peaches, peeled, pitted and coarsely chopped**
- 2 **nectarines, pitted and coarsely chopped**

Chapter 1: A–M

2 plums, pitted and coarsely chopped

In a medium skillet with a lid, melt the butter over medium heat and add the oil.

Add the shanks and saute them for 3 to 4 minutes on each side. Remove the shanks and set aside. Discard all but 2 tablespoon of fat from the pan. Stir constantly for 2 to 3 minutes to release any bits stuck to the pan.

Return to medium heat and add the onion and garlic. Saute 1 to 2 minutes, then add the bay leaf and thyme and sprinkle with the flour, turmeric and chili flakes. Stir for 1 to 2 minutes, then add the wine.

Add 1 1/2 cups of the chicken broth and return the shanks to the pan. Reduce the heat to low and cover.

Simmer for 1 1/2 hours, then add the fruit and continue to cook for another 45 minutes to 1 hour, until the meat is tender and can be pulled away from the bone. Stir occasionally while cooking, basting the shanks with the sauce.

As the sauce thickens, the sugar in the fruit will cause it to stick to the pan, so stir more frequently. Add more broth if necessary.

When the shanks are done, remove them from the pan and pull away or cut off the meat. Discard the bone. Skim the surface fat from the sauce.

Return the meat to the sauce and cook over low heat for 3 to 4 minutes, just enough to heat the meat through. Serve immediately.

Lamb Greats

GIGOT D'AGNEAU BONELESS LEG OF LAMB

4 servings
Source: Lamb Greats

- 1 leg of lamb -, (6 to 7 lbs), bone removed
- 12 garlic cloves
- 4 tablespoons **chopped fresh rosemary**
- 6 tablespoons **virgin olive oil**
- 3 tablespoons **sea salt**
- 3 tablespoons **freshly-cracked black pepper**

Preheat oven to 450°F. Butter open leg of lamb and set aside.

Place garlic, rosemary, olive oil, sea salt and pepper in a food processor and blend until smooth. Remove paste and smear all over inside and outside of lamb. Roll lamb up like a jelly roll and tie with butcher's twine. Place in a roasting pan and put into oven. Roast 45 to 50 minutes for medium-rare (internal temperature of 120 degrees). Remove and allow to rest 10 minutes before carving.

Serve with simple roasted potatoes, green beans and eggplant timbales.

HAMMIN DI PESACH (LAMB, MEATBALLS & SPINACH FOR PASSOVER)

1 servings
Source: Lamb Greats

- 1 **Chicken breast (2 halves) ground**
- 4 teaspoons **Olive oil**
- 1 **Egg, slightly beaten**
- 2 tablespoons **Matza meal***
- 8 cups **Chicken broth salt freshly**
- ground black pepper
- 1 ds Nutmeg
- 2 ½ lbs. **Lamb, breast of or rib chops**

Chapter 1: A-M

- 2 Garlic cloves, sliced
- 2 Parsley, Italian sprigs coarsely chopped
- 1 cup -Warm water
- 2 lbs. Spinach, cooked and slightly drained
- 4 Matzot; regular, broken into large pieces

* Matza meal and Matzots purchase in some superets and Jewish grocery stores.

(The word Hammin (or Hammim) is derived from the Hebrew adjective Ham or warm which describes certain dishes that are kept warm for prolonged periods of time...In Pitigliano, however Hammin was the classic one-course meal for Passover that both rich and poor used to make. The only difference between the versions was the in the cuts of meat used. Poor people used breast of lamb..and meatballs made with beef(when the cost of ground beef was a fraction of the cost of chicken.) People who didn't have to worry about the cost used tiny rib chops from baby lamb and chicken balls."

Combine ground chicken, 1 Tbsp olive oil, egg, matza meal and 2 Tbsp broth in small bowl. Add salt, pepper and nutmeg to taste and mix well. In large pot, place the lamb with remaining oil, sprinkle with tsp salt and 1/4 tsp pepper and lightly brown for 2-3 minutes. Add garlic, parsley and 1 cup of warm water. Form many tiny bowls with the ground chicken mixture and gently add to pot with lamb. Cover and simmer 1 to 1/2 hours.

Add spinach and 1 Tsp salt and simmer, covered, 15 minutes longer. Transfer the lamb chops, half the spinach and most of the gravy to a hot serving dish and keep warm. Add remaining broth to pot and bring to a boil. Add matza pieces and cook to 5 minutes. Turn the heat off and let stand 5 minutes before serving as a soup. Serve the lamb and spinach as the main dish.

SERVES: 6-8

HERB CRUSTED LEG OF LAMB

8 servings
Source: Lamb Greats

9 lbs. **leg of lamb, bone-in**

1 tablespoon **olive oil, plus**

¼ teaspoon **olive oil**

1 ½ teaspoons **salt**

½ teaspoon **freshly-ground black pepper**

1 **garlic head**

¼ cup **extra-virgin olive oil**

¼ cup **fresh lemon juice**

1 tablespoon **dried Greek oregano**

¾ cup **chopped flat-leaf parsley**

1 tablespoon **flour**

⅓ cup **brandy**

1 ½ cups **chicken stock**

1 tablespoon **chopped fresh rosemary**

Let lamb stand at room temperature for one hour. Heat oven to 325 degrees. Remove all but a thin layer of fat from lamb. Rub lamb with 1 tablespoon oil; sprinkle with 1 teaspoon salt and 1/4 teaspoon pepper. Place on a rack in a heavy roasting pan; place in oven.

Meanwhile, rub head of garlic with 1/4 teaspoon oil; wrap loosely in foil. Bake until garlic is very soft, about 1 hour. Let cool.

Cut off top of garlic head; squeeze roasted garlic into a bowl. Using a fork, mash garlic to a paste. Add extra-virgin olive oil, lemon juice, oregano, parsley, and remaining 1/2 teaspoon salt and 1/4 teaspoon pepper; mix well.

Rotate pan after lamb has roasted 1 1/4 hours. After 30 minutes more, slather lamb with roasted garlic paste. Roast an additional hour (for a total roasting time of about 2 3/4 hours), or until an instant-read thermometer inserted at the thickest part reads 160 degrees. Remove from oven and let rest 20 minutes.

Transfer lamb to a carving board. Pour off fat from roasting pan; place over medium-high heat. Sprinkle with flour and stir with a wooden spoon. Pour in brandy; scrape up brown bits from bottom of pan. Lower heat to medium; let liquid reduce by half. Add stock, stirring until incorporated. Add rosemary and salt and pepper to taste.

Slice lamb; serve with sauce on the side.

This recipe yields 8 to 10 servings.

INDIAN BRAISED LAMB

4 servings
Source: Lamb Greats

1 **yellow onion, chopped**

2 tablespoons **peeled and chopped fresh ginger**

3 **garlic cloves, chopped**

1 **small red or green jalapeno chili, seeded and minced**

1 tablespoon **ground coriander**

1 teaspoon **curry powder**

¼ teaspoon **ground cinnamon**

2 lbs. **boneless lamb shoulder, cut into large cubes**

2 teaspoons **salt, plus more, to taste**

3 tablespoons **corn or peanut oil**

2 cups **water**

1 cup **plain yogurt**

Steamed rice for serving

In a blender, combine the onion, ginger, garlic and chili and process until a paste forms. In a small bowl, stir together the coriander, curry powder and cinnamon. Set aside.

Season the lamb with 1 tsp. of the salt. Heat a Dutch oven or large, deep fry pan over high heat until very hot and add 2 Tbs. of the oil. Add the lamb in a single layer, working in batches if necessary to avoid crowding, and sear, turning once, until browned on all sides, 8 to 10 minutes. Using a slotted spoon, transfer the lamb to a plate.

Return the pan to medium heat and add the remaining 1 Tbs. oil. Add the onion-garlic paste and saute just until it begins to brown, about 3 minutes. Stir in the spice mixture and saute for 10 seconds more. Add the water and the remaining 1 tsp. salt. Increase the heat to medium-high and bring to a boil, then reduce the heat to low. Gradually whisk in the yogurt until combined with the sauce.

Return the lamb to the pan, cover and simmer gently until the lamb is tender, 60 to 70 minutes. Taste and adjust the seasonings with salt. Serve with steamed rice.

Comments: For a heartier dish, stir in 1/2 lb. boiling potatoes, peeled and cut into large cubes, during the last 20 minutes of cooking. The stew may be prepared up to 2 days in advance, covered and refrigerated; reheat over medium-low heat just before serving. It can also be frozen for up to 2 months.

INDIAN MUTTON CURRY (OR BEEF)

6 servings
Source: Lamb Greats

- 2 tablespoons **butter or margarine**
- 1 lb. **beef, trimmed, cubed**
- 1 **onion, sliced**
- 2 **potato, cut in 1" cubes**
- 1 **carrot, peeled and sliced**
- 1 cu **cauliflower florets**
- 1 cu **eggplant, cut in 1" cubes**
- 3 cloves **garlic, minced**
- 2 **green chiles, fresh**
- 2 tablespoons **coriander, ground**
- 1 tablespoon **chili powder**
- 1 teaspoon **ground cumin**

Chapter 1: A–M

1 teaspoon **ground ginger**

1 teaspoon **turmeric**

1 teaspoon **curry powder, or to taste**

1 tablespoon **mustard seed**

½ cup **white vinegar**

¾ cups **coconut milk**

To moderately hot butter in large skillet or wok, add onions, garlic, chilies, mustard seeds, curry powder, coriander powder, chili powder, cumin powder, turmeric powder, and ginger. Stir constantly, them lower heat.

Add beef and vegetables; saute until beef is browned , then add diluted coconut milk and vinegar.

Simmer on very low heat until meat is nearly tender. When vegetables and meat are tender, add rice flour mixed with a little water and salt. Add more water if necessary.

IRISH STEW

4 servings
Source: Lamb Greats

3 lbs. **boneless lamb shoulder or beef tri-tip**

Salt, to taste

Freshly-ground black pepper, to taste

4 carrots

2 **white turnips**

2 **onions**

3 tablespoons **shortening**

7 cups **boiling water**

2 **bay leaves, torn in half**

Cut meat into 1 1/2 inch cubes. Spread it on a piece of wax paper and salt and pepper pieces liberally. Set aside.

Peel carrots, slice them into 1/4-inch pieces and place in a bowl. Cut stem top and root bottom off turnips. Peel and slice into pieces about

41

1/4-inch thick. Add to carrots.

Cut stem top and root bottom off onions and, using a paring knife, peel the papery outside skin off and discard. Cut the onion in half horizontally. Put each half flat-side down on the cutting board and slice into 1/4-inch slices. Add onions to vegetables and set aside.

Melt shortening in large pot over medium-high heat and add meat. Brown well, 5 to 6 minutes, turning cubes over to brown on all sides. Standing back a bit from the pot, slowly add boiling water to meat. It will bubble up and turn a golden brown. Stir and reduce heat to medium-low.

Add half the carrots, turnips, onions and bay leaves, stir, and cover. Cook 30 minutes, then add remaining vegetables and bay leaves. Taste for salt and add if needed. Cover and cook until meat is tender and thoroughly cooked and vegetables are tender, 30 minutes more.

Serve hot. Serve with corn bread and finish the supper with warm applesauce sweetened with brown sugar and drizzled with cream. This is also good served with horseradish on the side.

ITALIAN BRAISED LAMB AND POTATOES

6 servings
Source: Lamb Greats

5 tablespoons **olive oil**

1 kg **lamb, lean boneless from t shoulder cut into 4cm pcs**

2 **brown onions**

½ **bunch Italian parsley,** leaves only

3 **garlic cloves crushed**

1 **capsicum red, cut into strip**

250 **lamb or beef stock**

500 g **potatoes, peeled and cut into** 4 cm pieces

60 g **pecorino, grated**

The potatoes should be yellow, waxy ones, such as Petrones or Desirees.

Heat half the oil in a large heavy pot. Brown lamb well in batches and, using a slotted spoon, remove to a plate. Add remaining oil. Add onion and cook until softened. Add parsley, garlic and capsicum. Return lamb to pot, stir and add stock and freshly ground pepper to taste. (Don't add salt yet as pecorino is a salty cheese) Reduce heat, cover, and simmer for 30 minutes.

Add potato and simmer for another 20 minutes, or until lamb is almost tender. Stir in cheese and cook for 10 minutes. Season with freshly ground pepper and salt to taste.

Best if cooked 1 - 2 days ahead and refrigerated. Like all casseroles, it will improve in flavour during the resting period. Great for entertaining, because it can be cooked well in advance, leaving you free to get on with the many chores involved in throwing a party.

JAPANESE LAMB FOR CROCKPOT

8 servings
Source: Lamb Greats

2 lbs. **lamb**

¼ cup **sauce, soy**

1 tablespoon **honey**

2 tablespoons **vinegar**

2 tablespoons **sherry**

2 **garlic cloves, crushed**

¼ teaspoon **ginger, ground**

1 ½ cups **stock, chicken, optional**

Put all ingredients in crockpot and cook all day on LOW.

This worked great on cheap stew lamb; it actually took away the strong lamb taste. I defatted the crockpot juices, thickened with cornstarch, and used it on green beans.

KADAI CHOP

4 servings
Source: Lamb Greats

8 lamb chops, (500g) (single bone)
oil for deep frying
FOR THE MARINADE
salt to taste
20 g **chile powder**
10 g **garam masala powder**
20 g **ginger paste**
30 g **garlic paste**
60 g **raw papaya paste**
10 g **black pepper powder**
30 **lemon juice**
FOR THE BATTER
100 g **cornstarch**
salt to taste
50 g **flour**
10 g **ginger paste**
20 g **garlic paste**

WASH and dry the lamb chops. Mix salt, chile powder, garam masala powder, ginger paste, garlic paste, raw papaya paste, black pepper powder and lemon juice well and apply to the chops. Keep aside for half an hour.

Mix all ingredients for the batter and add enough water to mix to a smooth paste of coating consistency. Dip the marinated chops in this batter and deep fry in hot oil until done. Serve hot.

KAKORI KABOB

4 servings
Source: Lamb Greats

500 g **boneless lamb, cubed**	25 g **cashew nuts**
200 g **kidney fat**	10 g **almonds**
50 g **raw papaya paste**	50 g **brown onion**
25 g **roasted chana, powdered**	25 g **raw red onion**
50 g **desi ghee**	salt to taste
FOR THE MARINADE	100 g **poppy seeds**
5 g **Kashmiri mirch powder**	10 g **chironji**
2 g **black pepper powder**	10 g **melon seeds**
1 g **green cardamom**	10 g **mawa**
2 g **black cardamom**	35 g **roasted chana, powdered**
1 1 g **clove powder**	100 g **desi ghee**
a pinch of **nutmeg powder**	a few strands **saffron**
a pinch of **mace powder**	a few drops **sweet ittar**
1 cm **cinnamon**	a few drops **gulab jal or**
a few **rose petals**	**kewra essence**

CLEAN the lamb cubes and mince. Add kidney fat and mince again seven to eight times. Add raw papaya paste to the mince, mix well and rest for a while.

Grind all the marinade ingredients to a paste and add to the mince. Mix well and keep aside for 30 minutes in a cold place. Add roasted chana powder and desi ghee. Mix well and refrigerate until the mixture is stiff.

Skewer on a greased kakori seekh with wet hands. Cook on a charcoal grill until done.

Lamb Greats

Serve hot with mint chutney, laccha pyaaz and sheermal.

KORMA - LAMB WITH CASHEW-NUT CURRY

4 servings
Source: Lamb Greats

¼ cup **unsalted cashews**

3 **dried hot red chilies**

1 **2 in piece stick cinnamon**

1 **1 in cube fresh ginger**

¼ teaspoon **cardamom seeds**

3 **whole cloves**

2 **large garlic cloves peeled**

2 tablespoons **poppy seed, (white)**

1 tablespoon **coriander seeds**

1 teaspoon **cumin seeds**

½ teaspoon **saffron threads**

6 tablespoons **ghee, (or melted butter)**

1 cup **chopped onion**

2 teaspoons **salt**

½ cup **unflavored yoghurt**

1 ½ lbs. **lamb cut into 2" cubes**

2 tablespoons **finely chopped coriander**

1 tablespoon **lemon juice**

¼ cup **boiling water**

1 cup **cold water**

To make the masala, combine the cashews, chilies, ginger and the cold water and blend at high speed for 1 minutes. Add the cinnamon, cardamom, cloves, garlic, poppy seeds, coriander seeds and cumin. Blend again until the mixture is completely pulverized. Set the masala aside. Place the saffron in a small bowl, pour in boiling water and let soak for at least 10 minutes.

In a heavy skillet heat the ghee over moderate heat until a drop of water flicked into it sputters instantly. Add the onions and, stirring constantly, fry for 7 or 8 minutes, until soft and golden brown. Stir in the salt and the masala, then add the yoghurt. Stirring occasionally, cook over moderate heat until the ghee lightly films the surface.

Add the lamb, turning it about with a spoon to coat the pieces evenly. Squeeze the saffron between your fingers, thin stir it and its soaking liquid into the skillet. Reduce the heat to low, cover tightly, and cook for 20 minutes, turning the lamb cubes over from time to time. Scatter 1/2 of the fresh coriander over the lamb and continue cooking, tightly covered for 10 minutes more, or until the lamb is tender. To serve, transfer the entire contents of the skillet to a heated platter, and sprinkle the top with lemon juice and the remaining fresh coriander.

LAMB AND APPLE CASSEROLE

4 servings
Source: Lamb Greats

2 lbs. **Middle neck of lamb**

8 ounces **Peeled onion**

1 lg **Cooking apple**

1 lb. **Potatoes**

1 ounce **Seedless raisins**

½ teaspoon **Mixed herbs**

Salt and pepper, to taste

2 teaspoons **Marmite**

½ pint **Hot water**

½ ounce **Butter or arine**

Trim the excess fat from the lamb and cut into neat portions.

Slice onions thinly.

Peel and core apple and cut into thin slices.

Peel potatoes and rinse under cold water. Slice thinly.

Cover base of a large casserole (about 3-pint size) with a layer of potato, followed by onions and apple. Add raisins and meat then sprinkle with herbs and a shake of salt and pepper. Top with remaining apple and onions then lastly with remaining potato slices.

Dissolve Marmite in the hot water and pour into a dish over vegetables and meat.

Dot top with small pieces of butter or margarine then cover with lid or aluminium foil.

Bake in centre of moderate oven (350°F or Gas No. 4) for 1-1/2 hours.

Uncover and continue to cook for further 20 to 30 minutes or until potatoes are golden.

LAMB AND PINE NUT STIR-FRY

2 servings
Source: Lamb Greats

4 ounces **Boneless lamb**

⅓ cup **Water**

1 tablespoon **Oyster sauce** *

1 ½ teaspoons **Cornstarch**

1 teaspoon **Grated gingerroot**

½ teaspoon **Instant chicken bouillon**

1 ½ cups **Bok choy, cut in 1" pieces**

½ cup **Sliced fresh mushrooms**

2 tablespoons **Water**

1 tablespoon **Cooking oil**

¼ cup **Pine nuts, toasted**

1 x Hot cooked rice (opt.)

Oyster sauce is an ingredient used frequently in Oriental Cooking. Partially freeze lamb. Thinly slice into bite-size strips.

In a -cup measure stir together 1/3 cup water, oyster sauce, cornstarch, grated gingerroot, and chicken bouillon granules. Micro-cook, uncovered, on 100% of power for 1 1/2 to 2 minutes or till thickened and bubbly, stirring every 30 seconds. Set aside.

In a small nonmetal bowl combine bok choy, sliced mushrooms, and 2 T water. Cover with vented clear plastic wrap. Micro-cook, covered, on 100% power 3 to 4 minutes or till bok choy is just crisp-tender. Drain. Cover and set aside.

Preheat a 6 1/2-inch microwave browning dish on 100% power for minutes. Add cooking oil to browning dish. Swirl to coat dish. Add lamb strips.

Micro-cook, covered, on 100% power for 1 1/2 to 2 /2 minutes or till lamb is done. Drain off fat. Stir in oyster sauce mixture with toasted pine nuts and bok choy mixture. Serve over hot cooked rice if desired.

LAMB APPETIZER

45 servings
Source: Lamb Greats

15 sl White bread
Butter or arine, melted
Celery seeds
1 cup **Ground cooked lamb**
¼ cup **Mayonnaise**
1 sm **Onion, minced**

¼ teaspoon **Paprika**
1 teaspoon **Lemon juice**
2 tablespoons **Chopped chives**
Pimiento strips, -=OR=-
 Parsley sprigs

Trim crusts from bread. Brush one side of each slice with melted butter and sprinkle with celery seeds. Cut each slice in 3 strips and place on baking sheet. Bake at 425°F 8 to 10 minutes. Blend lamb, Mayonnaise, onion, paprika, lemon juice and chives. Spread each toast strip with about 1 1/2 teaspoons meat mixture and garnish with pimiento strips.

Lamb Greats

LAMB BURGERS WITH SEPHARDIC CHAROSET

8 servings
Source: Lamb Greats

1 lb. **lean ground lamb**	½ cup **pitted dates, cut in half**
Salt, to taste	½ cup **dried apricots, cut in half**
Freshly-ground black pepper, to taste	1 **apple, unpeeled, cored, and diced**
1 tablespoon **oil**	½ teaspoon **ground allspice**
=== SEPHARDIC CHAROSET ===	½ cup **chopped walnuts**

For the Sephardic Charoset: Blend dates, apricots, apple and allspice in bowl of food processor until very finely minced. Add walnuts and pulse on and off until mixture is blended. Do not puree. Transfer to bowl, cover with plastic wrap and refrigerate 1 hour.

Combine lamb, Charoset and salt and pepper to taste in large bowl. Knead into ball, divide into 8 pieces and shape into patties. Heat oil in nonstick skillet over medium heat, and fry patties until crisp and brown on both sides, 3 to 4 minutes per side.

This recipe yields 8 servings.

Each serving: 237 calories; 64 mg sodium; 30 mg cholesterol; 15 grams fat; 18 grams carbohydrates; 9 grams protein; 0.97 gram fiber.

LAMB CHOP WITH JACKFRUIT GRAVY

4 servings
Source: Lamb Greats

2 rack lamb racks

olive oil to brush and baste braised- ***FOR THE FIRST MARINADE***

Chapter 1: A–M

2 teaspoons **chile powder**

30 g **salt or to taste, for rubbing**

7 teaspoons **ginger paste**

3 ½ teaspoons **garlic paste**

½ cup **red wine vinegar**

FOR THE STUDDING

12 **cloves**

12 **cloves garlic**

2 sticks **cinnamon**

16 **black peppercorns**

FOR THE BRAISING

oil for basting the legs

1 tablespoon **fresh basil leaves**

20 g **ginger**

5 **green cardamom**

2 **black cardamom**

3 **bay leaves**

12 **rose petals**

salt to taste

FOR THE SECOND MARINADE

4 tablespoons **curd, beaten**

60 g **processed cheese, grated**

¼ cup **cream**

1 ½ teaspoons **fresh basil leaves, chopped**

MIX FOR THE MASALA

¾ teaspoons **coarse black pepper powder**

½ teaspoon **amchur powder**

¼ teaspoon **kasoori methi powder**

¼ teaspoon **kebab cheeni, (allspice) powder**

a pinch of **rose petal powder**

a generous pinch **black salt**

FOR THE JACKFRUIT

600 g **kathael, (jackfruit)**

oil

MIX FOR THE MARINADE

2 teaspoons **lemon juice**

2 teaspoons **oil**

1 ½ teaspoons **chile powder**

1 teaspoon **turmeric powder**

salt to taste

oil for deep frying jackfruit and greasing the roasting tray

FOR THE GRAVY

6 tablespoons **ghee** –

2 **onions, grated**

3 ½ teaspoons **garlic paste**

2 ½ teaspoons **ginger paste**

2 teaspoons **coriander powder**

1 teaspoon **chile powder**

1 teaspoon **turmeric powder**

150 g **curd**

250 **fresh tomato puree**

100 g **fried onion paste**

salt to taste

4 cups **clear vegetable stock**

Lamb Greats

6 pandan, (fragrant screwpine) leaves (or 25 basil- leaves)

¾ teaspoons green cardamom powder

¼ teaspoon mace

a few strands saffron, soaked in lukewarm water and crushed to a paste

FOR THE GARNISH

15 g coriander leaves, chopped

To prepare the first marinade: FORCEFULLY rub – as in massage – the kid/lamb racks with chile powder. Repeat the process with salt, garlic paste, ginger paste and finally with vinegar. (Each of these ingredients is to be rubbed separately, and not as mixture). Refrigerate for 30 minutes. For the studding, using a cooking needle stud the fleshiest meat of the racks with garlic flakes and the spices.

For the braising, rub the racks with oil, arrange in a roasting tray, add the remaining ingredients and enough water to cover the racks. Braise in a preheated oven (400°F) until the liquor begins to boil. Lower the oven temperature to 150°F and braise for two-and-a-half hours. Remove and discard the liquor. Brush the racks with olive oil and keep aside.

To prepare the second marinade: Put all the ingredients in a bowl and whisk to mix well. Rub the olive oil-coated racks with this marinade and refrigerate for 30 minutes. (Remove at least 10 minutes before cooking) Skewer the rack pieces right down middle horizontally and as close to the bone as possible.

To prepare the kathael (jackfruit): Rub hands with oil. Peel the jackfruit, cut into quarters, core and cut into four cm chunks. Remove the seeds and keep aside. Rub the jackfruit cubes with the marinade and reserve for 15 minutes. Heat oil in a kadai, add the jackfruit pieces and deep fry over medium heat until light golden and done. Remove to an absorbent paper to drain the excess fat.

To prepare the gravy: Put curd, coriander powder, chile powder and turmeric powder in a bowl and whisk well. Clean, wash and pat dry the pandan (or basil) leaves. Heat ghee in a pan and fry the onions over medium heat until translucent. Add garlic paste and ginger paste. Stir-fry until the onions are light brown. Remove the pan from heat, stir in the curd mixture followed by tomato puree. Stir-fry after each addition until the ghee floats on top. Add the fried onion paste and stir-fry well. Add stock, pandan (or basil) leaves and salt. Bring to a boil.

Lower the heat and simmer, stirring occasionally, until reduced by half. When slightly cool, pass the gravy through a fine mesh soup strainer into a separate pan. Bring to a boil, lower the heat and simmer stirring occasionally until the gravy reaches thin sauce consistency. Sprinkle cardamom powder and mace powder. Add saffron and adjust the seasoning Arrange the fried jackfruit in a greased roasting tray, pour half the gravy over and cook in the preheated oven (200°F) for about ten minutes.

Roast the racks in a moderately hot tandoor for about six minutes. Remove, baste with olive oil and roast again for two minutes. Or, arrange leg on mesh of charcoal grill, cover and roast over moderate heat for about eight minutes, turning occasionally. Uncover, baste with oil and roast for two more minutes, turning once.

Baste racks with butter, arrange on a carving platter, sprinkle the masala over and serve hot.

LAMB CHOPS CREOLE

2 servings
Source: Lamb Greats

- 6 **shoulder lamb chops**
- 1 teaspoon **cooking oil**
- 1 medium **onion, diced**
- 1 ½ cups **green peppers, chopped**
- 2 ½ cups **canned tomatoes, drained**
- 2 ds **cayenne pepper**
- ½ teaspoon **chili powder**

Sprinkle a heavy frying pan with salt; brown the chops on both sides and put them in a casserole. Wipe out the skillet with a paper napkin or towel; put in the oil and heat. Add the onions and green pepper.

Brown lightly; then add tomatoes and seasoning. Stir the mixture well; simmer for a few minutes and then pour it over the lamb chops. Bake tightly covered for an hour at 350°F.

LAMB CHOPS WITH MOROCCAN SPICES

4 servings
Source: Lamb Greats

- ½ cup **chopped fresh mint, plus more for** garnish (optional)
- 1 tablespoon **ground coriander**
- 2 teaspoons **finely minced garlic**
- 1 teaspoon **sweet paprika**
- 1 teaspoon **ground cumin**
- 1 teaspoon **freshly ground black pepper**
- ¼ teaspoon **cayenne pepper**
- Salt, to taste
- Juice of 1 lemon
- 2 tablespoons **olive oil**
- 8 loin lamb chops or 16 small rib chops

In a small bowl, stir together the 1/2 cup mint, the coriander, garlic, paprika, cumin, black pepper, cayenne pepper, salt, lemon juice and olive oil. Rub the mixture into the chops, coating evenly, and place in a nonaluminum container. Cover and marinate at cool room temperature for 2 hours or up to overnight in the refrigerator.

Prepare a fire in a grill. If the chops are refrigerated, bring to room temperature.

Place the chops on an oiled grill rack and grill, turning once, for 4 minutes per side for medium-rare, or until done to your liking.

Transfer to a warmed platter or individual plates and sprinkle with mint, if using. Serve immediately.

LAMB CURRY WITH PUMPKIN

2 servings
Source: Lamb Greats

4 tablespoons **vegetable oil**

1 lb. **lean lamb shoulder meat, trimmed and cut into 1-inch cubes**

1 cup **chopped yellow onion**

3 **black or green cardamom pods**

2 **cassia leaves**

1 tablespoon **peeled and grated fresh ginger**

2 teaspoons **minced garlic**

2 tablespoons **ground coriander**

½ teaspoon **ground turmeric**

1 cup **chopped tomato**

1 tablespoon **tomato paste**

2 cups **chicken stock or water**

1 ½ teaspoons **salt, or to taste**

1-lb. piece **pumpkin or butternut squash, peeled, seeded and cut into 1-inch pieces**

1 tablespoon **garam masala (see related recipe at right)**

¼ cup **chopped fresh cilantro**

In a large, heavy, flameproof baking dish over high heat, warm 2 Tbs. of the oil. When hot, add a few pieces of the lamb and sear until they are lightly browned all over but not cooked through, about 3 minutes. Transfer to a bowl. Repeat with the remaining lamb.

Reduce the heat to medium-high and add the remaining 2 Tbs. oil to the baking dish. When hot, add the onion, cardamom and cassia leaves and cook, stirring occasionally, until the onion is browned, about 8 minutes. Stir in the ginger, garlic, coriander and turmeric.

Return the lamb to the baking dish along with the tomato, tomato paste, stock and salt.

Bring to a boil, then reduce the heat to low, cover and cook until the meat is tender when pierced with a fork, about 2 hours. Alternatively, place the covered baking dish in a preheated 350°F oven for 2 1/2 hours.

About 20 minutes before the meat is done, stir in the pumpkin, cover and continue cooking until the lamb and pumpkin are tender and cooked through.

Taste and adjust the seasonings. Transfer the curry to a warmed platter, taking care not to crush the pumpkin. Sprinkle with the garam masala and cilantro and serve immediately.

LAMB SHANKS WITH APRICOT COUSCOUS

4 servings
Source: Lamb Greats

4 Lamb shanks (3-4 lbs total) bones cracked

1 lg Onion, finely chopped

1 Cinnamon stick (2"long)

1 ½ teaspoons Ground coriander

1 teaspoon Ground ginger

½ teaspoon Ground cumin

¼ teaspoon Ground allspice

1 ¼ cups Chicken broth

¼ cup Apricot or orange muscat dessert wine

¾ cups Coarsely chop dried apricots

1 ½ cups Couscous

Mint sprigs (optional)

Place lamb shanks in a single layer in a shallow baking pan. Bake in a 450 oven until well browned (20-25 minutes). Meanwhile, in a 4 quart or larger electric slow cooker, combine onion, cinnamon stick, coriander, ginger, cumin and all spice. Lift lamb from baking pan and place on top of onion mixture; discard fat in pan. Pour broth over lamb. Cover and cook at low setting until lamb is so tender it pulls away from bones when prodded with a fork (7 1/2-9 hrs.)

Lift lamb to a warm, deep platter and keep warm. Skim and discard fat from cooking liquid; then measure liquid. You need 2 1/4 cups; if necessary, pour off some of the liquid or add enough hot water to make 2 1/4 cups. Return liquid to cooker and increase heat setting to high. Stir in wine and apricots, then couscous. Cover and let stand until liquid has been absorbed (about 10 more minutes.) Spoon couscous around lamb; garnish with mint, if desired.

"Fragrant apricot wine echoes the sweet-tart tang of dried apricots in a fluffy couscous to serve with spicy braised lamb shanks. To bring all the flavors together, steam the couscous in the liquid that remains in the cooker after the meat is done."

LAMB SHANKS WITH ARTICHOKES AND OLIVES

4 servings
Source: Lamb Greats

4 large fleshy lamb shanks

salt, to taste

freshly-ground black pepper, to taste

6 tablespoons **virgin olive oil**

1 **spanish onion, chopped 1/4" dice**

12 **garlic cloves, peeled, left whole**

2 tablespoons **freshly-chopped rosemary leaves**

12 **baby artichokes, outer leaves trimmed in acidulated water**

½ cup **gaeta olives**

1 cup **dry white wine**

1 cup **basic tomato sauce, see * note**

Lamb Greats

1 cup **chicken stock**   see * note

soft polenta with lemon,

Preheat oven to 375°F.

Rinse and dry shanks and season liberally with salt and pepper. In a heavy-bottomed Dutch oven with a lid, heat olive oil until smoking. Sear shanks until dark golden-brown over medium heat, about 15 to 18 minutes. Remove shanks and set aside.

Add onion, garlic, rosemary and artichokes and cook until softened, about 8 to 10 minutes. Add olives, wine, Basic Tomato Sauce and chicken stock and bring to a boil. Replace lamb shanks in pan and return to boil. Cover tightly and place in oven and cook for 1 1/2 hours, until fork tender. Remove and serve with Soft Polenta With Lemon, Thyme And Carrots.

LAMB TAGINE WITH ARTICHOKES AND MINT

6 servings
Source: Lamb Greats

3 lbs. (1.5 kg) boneless lamb shoulder or leg roast

2 tablespoons (25 mL) olive oil

2 onions, sliced

1 carrot, diced

4 cloves garlic, minced

2 teaspoons (10 mL) crumbled dried mint

1 teaspoon (5 mL) ground cumin

¼ cup (50 mL) dry white wine

1-½ cup (375 mL) chicken stock

1 bay leaf

½ teaspoon (2 mL) salt

¼ teaspoon (1 mL) pepper

1 can (19 oz/540 mL) chickpeas, drained and rinsed

1 can (14 oz/398 mL) artichokes, drained and quartered

Chapter 1: A-M

¼ cup (50 mL) raisins

1 teaspoon (5 mL) grated lemon rind

1 tablespoon (15 mL) lemon juice

¼ cup (50 mL) pine nuts

Preheat oven to 350°F (180°C).

Trim roast and cut into 1-inch (2.5 cm) cubes. In large Dutch oven, heat oil over medium-high heat; brown lamb in batches. Transfer to plate.

Drain any fat from pan and reduce heat to medium; cook onions, carrot, garlic, mint and cumin, stirring, until onions are softened, about 5 minutes. Add wine; cook, stirring, for 1 minute. Add chicken stock, bay leaf, salt and pepper.

Return lamb and any accumulated juices to pan; bring to boil.

Cover and simmer over medium-low heat, or cover and cook in oven, for 1 hour.

Stir in chickpeas, artichokes, raisins and lemon rind and juice; cover and cook until lamb is tender and sauce is thickened, about 30 minutes. Discard bay leaf.

Meanwhile, in small skillet, toast pine nuts over medium heat, shaking often, until golden, about 3 minutes; sprinkle over stew.

LAMB TAGINE WITH CHICKPEAS AND RAISINS, BASMATI RICE, HARIS

4 servings
Source: Lamb Greats

2 lbs. **lamb shoulder, cut 2" pieces**

6 **garlic cloves, coarsely chopped**

1 tablespoon **honey**

Lamb Greats

¼ cup **olive oil**

3 tablespoons **chopped cilantro**

1 pn **saffron threads**

2 teaspoons **paprika**

2 teaspoons **ground cumin**

2 tablespoons **sun-dried tomato paste**

Salt, to taste

Freshly-ground black pepper, to taste

2 **potatoes, cut into chunks**

2 **carrots, cut into chunks**

2 **yellow onions, peeled, and cut into chunks**

1 ½ cups **vegetable stock**

1 **cinnamon stick**

1 cup **cooked chickpeas**

½ cup **golden raisins**

=== HARISSA ===

2 **red bell peppers, roasted, peeled, and chopped**

1 small **red chile, chopped**

2 **garlic cloves, chopped**

½ tea pon **coriander seeds, toasted in a pan**

½ teaspoon **cumin**

Salt, to taste

3 tablespoons **olive oil**

=== BASMATI RICE ===

2 tablespoons **olive oil**

1 **yellow onion, finely chopped**

1 teaspoon **cumin seeds**

1 **cinnamon stick**

2 **cardamom seeds, crushed**

2 **bay leaves**

2 cups **basmati rice, washed well, drained**

3 cups **water**

2 tablespoons **lemon juice**

Salt, to taste

Freshly-ground black pepper, to taste

Tagine:

Mix together the garlic, honey, olive oil, cilantro, saffron, paprika, cumin and tomato paste in a large bowl. Add the lamb and toss to coat. Cover and marinate in the refrigerator overnight. Remove from the refrigerator 30 minutes before cooking.

Preheat oven to 400°F. Put the meat and the marinade into a tagine or Dutch oven and sprinkle with salt and pepper. Add the potatoes, carrots, onions, stock and cinnamon and stir together. Place the tagine or Dutch oven lid on and bake for 1 hour.

Stir the chickpeas and raisins into the tagine and cook for 30 minutes. Remove the lid or foil and cook an additional 30 minutes to brown the vegetables. Garnish with cilantro springs.

Harissa:

Combine all ingredients in a food processor and process until smooth.

Basmati Rice:

Heat oil in a medium saucepan over medium heat. Add the onions and cook until soft. Add the cumin seeds, cinnamon stick, cardamom seeds and bay leaves and cook for 2 to 3 minutes.

Add the rice and toss to coat with the mixture. Add the water and lemon juice and season with salt and pepper. Bring to a boil, cover and reduce heat to medium-low, cook for 15 minutes, or until rice is tender and water has been absorbed. Remove from the heat and leave covered for 5 minutes.

Fluff with a fork.

LAMB TAGINE WITH POTATOES AND CHICKPEAS

4 servings
Source: Lamb Greats

- 3 teaspoons **cumin seeds**
- 3 teaspoons **coriander seeds**
- ¾ teaspoons **peppercorns**
- 1 ½ teaspoons **sweet paprika**
- 1 teaspoon **ground ginger**
- 2 teaspoons **salt, plus more, to taste**
- 2 tablespoons **extra-virgin olive oil**

Lamb Greats

- 2 ½ lbs. **boneless leg of lamb, cut into 1-inch cubes**
- 1 **yellow onion, julienned**
- 4 **garlic cloves, minced**
- ¼ cup **water**
- ½ lb. **small Yukon Gold potatoes, halved**
- ¼ cup **chopped fresh cilantro,** plus more for garnish
- 1 can (15 oz.) **chickpeas, rinsed and drained**
- ¼ cup **fresh lemon juice**
- **Freshly ground pepper, to taste**
- **Cooked couscous for serving**

In a small fry pan over medium-low heat, toast the cumin and coriander seeds, stirring frequently, until fragrant, about 5 minutes. Transfer to a spice grinder, add the peppercorns, paprika, ginger and the 2 tsp. salt and grind until well combined. Set aside.

In a tagine over medium-high heat, warm 1 Tbs. of the olive oil until almost smoking. Working in batches, brown the lamb on all sides, 3 to 4 minutes total. Transfer to a plate.

Add the remaining 1 Tbs. oil and the onion to the tagine, reduce the heat to medium and cook, stirring, until translucent, 8 to 10 minutes. Add the garlic and the spice mixture, reduce the heat to medium-low and cook, stirring occasionally, until the onion is caramelized, about 2 minutes more. Add the lamb, water, potatoes and the 1/4 cup cilantro and bring to a simmer. Cover the tagine and adjust the heat so the mixture gently simmers. Cook for 45 minutes, then add the chickpeas and lemon juice. Continue cooking until the lamb is tender, about 45 minutes more. Taste and adjust the seasonings with salt and pepper.

Garnish with cilantro and serve the lamb directly from the tagine. Accompany with couscous.

Comments: To intensify their flavor, toast the cumin and coriander seeds in a dry fry pan before grinding them. Be sure to stir frequently and watch the spices closely so they don't burn.

LAMB TANDOORI

8 servings
Source: Lamb Greats

1 boneless leg of lamb, 3 to 4 lb., butterflied to 1 1/2-inch thickness
Salt and freshly ground pepper, to taste
½ cup **tandoori paste**
Lemon wedges for garnish
Naan or other flatbread for serving
Raita potato salad for serving

Season the lamb on both sides with salt and pepper. Cover with plastic wrap and refrigerate for 30 minutes.

Place the lamb in a vacuum marinator and add the tandoori paste. Create a vacuum seal and marinate on the tumble setting for 20 minutes according to the manufacturers instructions. When the marinator stops, reset it for 20 minutes more.

Prepare a medium-hot fire in a grill.

Place the lamb on the grill and cook, turning once, until an instant-read thermometer inserted into the thickest part of the meat registers 135°F for medium, 10 to 12 minutes per side, or until done to your liking.

Transfer the lamb to a carving board, cover loosely with aluminum foil and let rest for 5 to 10 minutes. Cut the meat into thin slices, arrange on a warmed platter and garnish with lemon wedges. Serve with naan and raita potato salad.

Comments: Ask your butcher to butterfly the leg of lamb into one large piece. This makes the cut even and allows for relatively quick cooking on the grill.

LAMB WITH ARUGULA DIPPING SAUCE

4 servings
Source: Lamb Greats

2 cups **arugula, trimmed**	some for drizzling
½ cup **smoked almonds**	8 **lamb chops**
1 **shallot, chopped**	**Grill seasoning, to taste**
½ cup **extra-virgin-olive oil, plus**	= (or coarse salt and pepper)
	1 cup **prepared mint jelly**

Preheat grill pan over high heat.

Combine arugula, almonds and shallot in food processor. Pulse-grind mixture. Turn processor on and stream in extra-virgin olive oil. Transfer mixture to a small bowl.

Drizzle chops with extra-virgin olive oil. Season with grill seasoning or salt and pepper and grill 3 minutes on each side. Transfer chops to a platter and serve with dipping sauce and mint jelly.

This recipe yields 4 servings.

LAMB WITH BUTTER BEANS

1 servings
Source: Lamb Greats

BUTTER BEANS

150 g **butter beans, washed, soaked overnight in plenty of**

cold water (OR 14 oz can of butterbeans, drained and washed.)

600 cold water

1 ¼ teaspoons **salt or to taste**

1 tablespoon **ginger paste**

2 teaspoons **garlic paste**

5 tablespoons **cooking oil**

2 **medium onions, finely chopped**

2 **dried red chillies, up to 3**

2 **cinnamon sticks, each 2" long, broken**

SPICE PASTE

1 ½ teaspoons **ground coriander**

2 ½ teaspoons **ground cumin**

1 teaspoon **ground turmeric**

½ teaspoon **chilli powder or to taste**

LAMB

1 kg **leg or shoulder of lamb, fat trimmed and cut into 1.25 inch cubes**

2 tablespoons **tomato puree**

2 **black cardamoms, split open the top of each pod, up to 3**

6 **whole cloves**

175 **warm water**

half a lemon, juice of

2 tablespoons **chopped coriander leaves**

Spice Paste: Make a paste of the Paste ingredients by adding 3 tbsp water.

Butter beans: Put the cold water and the butter beans in a sauce and bring the liquid to the boil. Partially cover the pan and cook over a low heat for 15 minutes.

Now cover the pan tightly and simmer the beans for about 20 minutes. Remove the pan from the heat and keep aside.

Heat oil over medium heat and add the onions, red chillies and cinnamon sticks. Stir and fry until the onions are soft, about 5 minutes.

Add the ginger and garlic pastes and stir and fry for 2-3 minutes.

Add the spice paste, adjust heat to low, stir and fry for a further 3-4 minutes.

Lamb: Add the meat, turn heat up to medium-high and fry for 5-6 minutes, stirring frequently. Stir in the tomato puree then add cardamoms, cloves and warm water. Bring to the boil, cover and simmer until the meat is tender, 55-60 minutes.

If using fresh butter beans add them, and the liquid in which they were cooked. Bring the liquid to the boil, cover the pan and simmer for 15 minutes. For canned butter beans simply add and simmer for 5 minutes.

Remove the pan from the heat and add the lemon juice and coriander leaves.

Serve with plain boiled rice or plain fried rice or Naan, Tandoori Roti etc.

LAMB WITH HONEY AND CUMIN

6 servings
Source: Lamb Greats

3 lbs. **lamb**

salt, to taste

freshly-ground black pepper, to taste

¼ cup **flour, for dredging**

6 tablespoons **extra-virgin olive oil**

1 **large spanish onion, cut 1/2" dice**

1 **green bell pepper, seeded, stemmed,** and chopped into 1/2" dice

1 tablespoon **hot paprika**

1 teaspoon **saffron**

2 tablespoons **currants**

4 tablespoons **sherry vinegar**

3 tablespoons **honey**

1 tablespoon **cumin seed**

2 cups **dry white wine**

1 cup **chicken stock**

Cut lamb into 2-inch cubes, season and dredge in flour. In a 4-quart casserole, heat oil until smoking. Brown lamb pieces until dark golden brown, 4 or 5 at a time, and hold on a plate.

Add onion, bell pepper, paprika, saffron and currants and cook until very soft, about 10 to 12 minutes. Add vinegar, honey, cumin, wine and stock and bring to a boil.

Add lamb pieces, return to boil, lower heat and simmer 1 hour 20 minutes, stirring every 20 minutes. Serve warm in bowls with grilled bread.

LEG OF LAMB WITH GARLIC & HERBS

6 servings
Source: Lamb Greats

½ cup **chopped mixed fresh herbs,**

such as

rosemary, thyme and oregano

¼ cup **chopped garlic**

2 teaspoons **lemon zest**

1 teaspoon **salt, plus more, to taste**

5 tablespoons **extra-virgin olive oil**

Freshly ground pepper,

to taste

1 bone-in leg of lamb, 5 to 6 lb., trimmed of

excess fat

20 fresh rosemary sprigs

5 heads of garlic, 1/4 inch cut off the top

¼ cup **Madeira**

2 cups **beef stock**

Position a rack in the lower third of an oven and preheat to 450°F.

In a small bowl, combine the mixed herbs, chopped garlic, lemon zest, the 1 tsp. salt, 3 Tbs. of the olive oil and pepper. Coat the lamb with the mixture.

In a large roasting pan over medium-high heat, warm the remaining 2 Tbs. oil. Add the lamb and brown, 3 to 4 minutes per side. Transfer to a platter.

Arrange the rosemary in the center of the pan. Place the lamb, fat side up, on top. Arrange the garlic heads around the lamb. Roast until an instant-read thermometer inserted into the thickest part of the meat, away from the bone, registers 130°F for medium-rare, about 1 hour. Transfer the lamb to a carving board, cover loosely with aluminum foil and let rest for 20 minutes.

Skim the fat from the pan, set over medium heat and add the Madeira, stirring to scrape up the browned bits from the pan bottom and smash the roasted garlic. Add the stock. Strain the sauce into a saucepan, set over medium heat and cook until thickened, 5 to 10 minutes. Taste and adjust the seasonings with salt and pepper.

Carve the lamb into thin slices and arrange on a warmed platter. Pass the sauce alongside.

Comments: To create a delicious sauce after roasting the lamb, this recipe employs a technique known as deglazing. When meat is roasted in a pan, the caramelizing process produces a fond, a coating of browned bits on the pan bottom. After the meat is removed, the pan is deglazed by adding wine, stock or other liquid. The liquid is heated and the cook stirs and scrapes with a wooden spoon to release the browned bits, which add depth of flavor to the finished sauce.

LIGHT STEW

6 servings
Source: Lamb Greats

1 tablespoon **Vegetable oil**

1 lb. 6 oz **lean boneless lamb, cut into 1 1/2" squares 1/2" thick (or boneless chuck)**

1 md **Onion, chopped**

Chapter 1: A-M

- 3 cups **Low sodium chicken broth**
- ½ teaspoon **Dried thyme, crumbled**
- 1 **Bay leaf**
- 6 5 oz **whole new red potatoes**
- 15 ounces **Small onions, peeled**
- 1 cup **h ale or beer**
- 1 teaspoon **Salt**
- 2 tablespoons **Cornstarch**
- **Chopped parsley**
- 6 1 oz **sliced Italian bread** (optional)

In a large heavy saucepan, heat 1/2 of the oil. Add 1/2 of the lamb or beef and cook until well browned on one side, 5-7 min. Stir and cook 1 minute longer; remove meat and set aside. Add the remaining oil the lamb (or beef) and the chopped onion to the pan and cook until browned, about 8-10 min. Return the first batch of meat to the pan.

Add broth and bring to a boil over medium heat. Add thyme and bay leaf; lower heat to low, and simmer for 1 hour.

Add potatoes, onions, ale and salt. Cover and simmer until potatoes are tender, 30-40 minutes.

To thicken stew, add cornstarch to 1/4 cup cold water in a small bowl; stir until smooth. Add to simmering stew; stir gently until thickened. Garnish with parsley; serve with bread.

LIULA-KABOB

8 servings
Source: Lamb Greats

- 4 lbs. **lean ground lamb**
- 12 tablespoons **mint leaves, (fresh), or-**
- 6 tablespoons **dried mint leaves**
- 4 teaspoons **salt**
- ½ cup **onion chopped fine**
- 12 **scallions, chopped**

Lamb Greats

1 tablespoon **black pepper ground**

2 **garlic cloves minced**

½ tablespoon **ginger ground**

1 tablespoon **red pepper flakes**

Make a layer of charcoal that has burned to a gray, hot coal. Mix in a large bowl the lamb and other ingredients. Beat with a wooden spoon until mixture is smooth.

Form this mixture into "sausages" approx 3" long and 2" in diameter.

Prepare grill.

Thread these "sausages" onto wooden skewers leaving a 1" space between the "sausages" then grill until done over the coals, usually about 12-15 minutes.

LOUBIA

8 servings
Source: Lamb Greats

2 cups **dried navy beans**

8 cups **water**

2 **bay leaves**

3 **onions**

4 cloves **whole**

5 cloves **garlic, minced**

1 **bone from a leg of lamb**

(or 1 lb of lamb bones)

2 tablespoons **olive oil**

8 **tomatoes, peeled, seeded, and chopped**

(or two 14 1/4-oz cans diced tomatoes)

2 tablespoons **tomato paste**

2 teaspoons **ground cumin**

1 tablespoon **sweet Hungarian paprika**

⅛ teaspoon **cayenne pepper, (optional)**

20 **cilantro sprigs**

30 **parsley sprigs**

3 teaspoons **salt** - (to 4 tspns)

Freshly-ground black pepper, to taste

Chapter 1: A-M

Chopped cilantro, for garnish

Chopped onion, for garnish

Chopped green olives, for garnish

Bread, for serving

Soak navy beans in water overnight; drain. Place drained navy beans, water, bay leaves, 1 onion studded with all 4 cloves, garlic and lamb bones in soup pot. Cover and cook over medium heat until beans are fairly soft, 1 to 1 1/2 hours. Discard onion.

Dice remaining onions. Heat oil in skillet over medium heat. Add onions and fry, stirring occasionally, until soft, 3 to 4 minutes. Add to cooked beans, along with 1/2 tomatoes, tomato paste, cumin, paprika and cayenne.

In blender or food processor, puree remaining 1/2 tomatoes with cilantro and parsley sprigs. Add to beans and cook over low heat, covered, until beans are tender and broth acquires full-bodied flavor, 1 to 1 1/2 hours. Season with salt and pepper to taste.

Ladle into individual bowls and garnish with cilantro, chopped onion and olives. Serve with warm bread.

This recipe yields 6 to 8 servings.

Each of 8 servings: 267 calories; 1,052 mg sodium; 0 cholesterol; 5 grams fat; 45 grams carbohydrates; 14 grams protein; 4.50 grams fiber.

MARINATED LAMB-AND-VEGETABLE KEBABS

8 servings
Source: Lamb Greats

2 lbs. **lean boneless leg of lamb**

¼ cup **red wine vinegar**

¼ cup **fresh lemon juice**

2 tablespoons **minced fresh parsley**

½ teaspoon **pepper**

Lamb Greats

½ teaspoon **ground cumin**

¼ teaspoon **salt**

3 cloves **garlic, minced**

1 unpeeled eggplant, (1 pound)

1 medium zucchini, (1/2 pound)

1 large sweet onion, cut into 8 wedges

1 medium red bell pepper, cut into 8 pieces

1 medium yellow bell pepper, cut into 8 pieces

8 large fresh mushrooms

Vegetable cooking spray

Trim fat from lamb, and cut lamb into 24 (2-inch) cubes.

Combine vinegar and next 6 ingredients in a large zip-top heavy-duty plastic bag. Add lamb cubes, and marinate in refrigerator 8 hours, turning bag occasionally.

Cut eggplant lengthwise into quarters. Cut each quarter crosswise into 4 pieces. Cut zucchini lengthwise in half. Cut each half crosswise into 4 pieces. Thread 2 eggplant pieces, 1 zucchini piece, and 1 onion wedge onto each of 8 (10-inch) skewers.

Remove lamb from bag, reserving marinade. Thread 3 lamb cubes, 1 red bell pepper piece, 1 yellow bell pepper piece, and 1 mushroom alternately onto each of 8 (10-inch) skewers.

Coat grill rack with cooking spray; place on grill over medium-hot coals. Place eggplant kebabs on rack, and cook 15 minutes, basting with reserved marinade. Turn eggplant kebabs, and cook 7 minutes. Add lamb kebabs to rack, and cook 4 minutes on each side or to desired degree of doneness, basting with reserved marinade. Yield: 8 servings (serving size: 1 eggplant kebab and 1 lamb kebab).

MAUSHAWA (PULSE AND YOGHURT SOUP)

1 servings
Source: Lamb Greats

2 ounces **chickpeas**

2 ounces **red kidney beans**

15 fluid ounces oz **yoghurt**

2 ounces **mung beans, (or green split**

peas)

1 2 oz **sho grain rice**

2 qt **water including the water**

for soaking the pulses

2 teaspoons **powdered dill**

salt

for the meat stew

8 ounces **beef, veal or lamb (cut in**

½ " **cubes)**

4 ounces **finely chopped onion**

3 tablespoons **vegetable oil**

2 ounces **tomatoes, skinned and**

chopped

⅓ pint **water**

¼ teaspoon **red pepper, up to 1**

salt

In Afghanistan this soup is served either as a stater or as a main meal. This is the original version of Maushawa, cooked with meat qorma but another popular version is made using meatballs (Kofta). The meatball are prepared as for the kofta in kofta chalau, but are smaller (about 1/2" or 1 cm in diameter). The sauce remains the same too, except that the yoghurt should be omitted. Afghans like to serve this soup "hot", but seasoning can be adjusted according to the taste.

Soak the chick peas and red kidney beans in water overnight. Drain the yoghurt for about an hour to make chaka. Put the chickpeas, red kidney beans, mung beans (or green split peas) and rice in large pan with 2 pint of water, including the water in which the pulses have been soaked. Bring to the boil, cover leaving the lid slightly ajar, turn the heat to low and simmer. Cook until the pulses are soft (the time this takes depends on the freshness of the pulses).

Meanwhile cook the meat and sauce. Heat the vegetable oil in a pan

Lamb Greats

and add the chopped onion. Fry over a medium heat until soft and reddish-brown. Add the meat and fry again until brown. Add the tomatoes, stirring well and boil for a minutes or so. Add the 1/4 pint water, the slat and re pepper. Stir well and bring back to the boil. Turn down the heat and simmer until the meat is tender and the sauce thickened.

When cooked, mix all the ingredients; the rice, chickpeas, red kidney beans, together with the juices in which they have cooked, the meat stew, the chaka, powdered dill and salt to taste. Stir well and add extra water if you want to thin the soup. Continue stirring and simmer for another 5-10 minutes to allow the flavours to blend.

Serve the Maushawa hot in individual soup plates or cups. Nan is usually served with this soup.

MOROCCAN LAMB TAGINE WITH RAISINS, ALMONDS, AND HONEY

6 servings
Source: Lamb Greats

* 2 teaspoons ras-el-hanout*
* 2 teaspoons salt
* 3/4 teaspoon black pepper
* 3/4 teaspoon ground ginger
* 1/4 teaspoon crumbled saffron threads
* 3 cups water
* 3 lb boneless lamb shoulder, cut into 1-inch cubes
* 1 large onion, coarsely grated (1 cup)
* 2 garlic cloves, finely chopped
* 2 (3-inch) cinnamon sticks
* 1/2 stick (1/4 cup) unsalted butter, cut into pieces
* 1 1/4 cups raisins
* 1 1/4 cups whole blanched almonds
* 1/2 cup honey
* 1 teaspoon ground cinnamon

*Accompaniment: couscous

Whisk together ras-el-hanout, salt, pepper, ginger, saffron, and 1 cup water in a 5-quart heavy pot. Stir in lamb, remaining 2 cups water, onion, garlic, cinnamon sticks, and butter and simmer, covered, until lamb is just tender, about 1 1/2 hours.

Stir in raisins, almonds, honey, and ground cinnamon and simmer, covered, until meat is very tender, about 30 minutes more.

Uncover pot and cook over moderately high heat, stirring occasionally, until stew is slightly thickened, about 15 minutes more.

Author Note: Cooks' note: iTagine can be made 1 day ahead and cooled, uncovered, then chilled, covered.

MOROCCAN SPICED MEATBALLS W/ EGGS IN TOMATO SAUCE

4 servings
Source: Lamb Greats

--Meatballs---

1 lb. **ground lamb or ground beef**

½ **onion, grated**

½ teaspoon **salt**

¼ teaspoon **pepper**

½ teaspoon **sweet Hungarian paprika**

2 sprigs fresh coriander, finely chopped

2 sprigs flat leaf parsley, finely chopped

--Sauce---

2 tablespoons **olive oil**

½ **onion, grated**

½ teaspoon **salt**

½ teaspoon **sweet Hungarian paprika**

⅛ teaspoon **ground ginger**

¼ teaspoon **turm**

½ teaspoon **cayenne pepper**

3 tablespoons **tomato paste**

1 cup **lamb stock or beef stock**

--Vegetables and Eggs---

Lamb Greats

2 cups **squash or potatoes, peeled & cut into large chunks**

½ cup **peas**

3 **eggs, beaten**

Use your hands to mix the meatball ingredients, and roll mixture into mini meatballs 3/4"-1" in diameter; set aside.

In a skillet or tajine combine sauce ingredients and let mixture simmer, covered, over low heat for 5 minutes.

Add meatballs, squash, and peas to the sauce and simmer, covered, over medium-low heat for 15 minutes.

Pour the eggs in in a stream over everything.

Cover and cook just long enough to cook the egg (about 3 minutes, depending on how well done you like your eggs).

Serve warm over couscous, sprinkled with cumin or black pepper if desired.

MOROCCAN-STYLE MEATBALLS

Servings: --
Source: Lamb Greats

2 tablespoons **olive oil**

1 **red onion, very finely chopped**

1 lb. **ground lamb**

3 **large garlic cloves, crushed through a press**

2 **eggs, lightly beaten**

1 cup **loosely packed fresh flat-leaf parsley leaves, finely chopped**

1 cup **loosely packed fresh mint leaves, finely chopped, plus sprigs for garnish**

- 2 tablespoons **fine dried bread crumbs**
- 1 ½ teaspoons **ground cumin**
- 1 teaspoon ground cinnamon
- 1 teaspoon **salt, plus more, to taste**
- ½ teaspoon **freshly ground pepper,** plus more, to taste
- **Lemon wedges for squeezing and garnish**
- About 42 cocktail picks (optional)

Lightly oil a shallow-rimmed baking sheet.

In a fry pan over medium-low heat, warm the olive oil. Add the onion and sautÈ, stirring occasionally, until very soft, about 10 minutes. Transfer to a large bowl and let cool.

Add the lamb, garlic, eggs, parsley, chopped mint, bread crumbs, cumin, cinnamon, the 1 tsp. salt and the 1/2 tsp. pepper to the bowl with the onion. Combine the ingredients thoroughly with your hands (the only way to evenly distribute the ingredients). Fry a small pinch of the mixture, taste, and adjust the seasonings with salt and pepper. Form the mixture into balls about the size of a walnut, rolling them very lightly in the palms of your hands. Place on the prepared baking sheet.

Preheat a broiler. Place the meatballs about 4 inches from the heat source and broil, turning once with tongs, until brown and crispy on both sides, about 10 minutes total. Remove the baking sheet from the broiler and transfer the meatballs to a platter.

Squeeze some lemon juice over the meatballs and arrange the remaining lemon wedges and mint sprigs on the platter. Using a cocktail pick, skewer each meatball. Serve immediately.

Comments: Although these meatballs are not a traditional dish of Morocco, the presence of mint, parsley, cinnamon and cumin gives them a strong North African accent. Use a light hand when forming the balls, just as you would when shaping a hamburger patty. A gentle touch ensures that the meat is not compacted or overheated by contact with your hands, resulting in light, tender mouthfuls. If doubling this recipe, use only 1 1/2 times the amount of salt, not double the amount.

Author Note: Note: The meatballs can be refrigerated for up to 4 hours before cooking. Remove them from the refrigerator 15 minutes before cooking. If desired, cook and cool the meatballs, refrigerate them for up to 4 hours, and then reheat in a 350°F oven until heated through, 10 to 20 minutes.

MOUSSAKA (LAMB AND EGGPLANT CASSEROLE)

6 servings
Source: Lamb Greats

4 7" **eggplants, washed (7 to 8)**

1 tablespoon **salt**

2 tablespoons **olive oil**

2 lbs. **lean ground lamb**

vegetable oil

⅔ cups **finely chopped onion**

8 ounces **sliced mushrooms, drained**

1 teaspoon **salt**

1 teaspoon **dried rosemary leaves**

½ teaspoon **dried thyme leaves**

1 **clove garlic, peeled crushed**

⅔ cups **beef stock or broth**

1 ½ teaspoons **cornstarch**

3 tablespoons **tomato paste, (save remainder for**

3 **eggs, slightly beaten**

tomato sauce for moussaka, (recipe)

Remove green caps from eggplants and slice eggplants in half lengthwise. Make deep slashes in eggplant pulp, but do not cut through skins. Sprinkle eggplant halves with the 1 tablespoon salt and allow to stand at room temperature 1/2 hour.

Squeeze moisture out of eggplant halves and brush cut surfaces with the 2 tablespoons of olive oil. Heat 4 eggplant halves at a time in Microwave Oven 7 minutes or until pulp is tender. Repeat with remaining eggplant halves.

Scoop pulp out of eggplant, being careful not to rip skins. Set skins aside. Chop eggplant pulp coarsely. Place pulp in a medium-sized, heat-resistant, non-metallic bowl and heat, un- covered, in Microwave Oven 4 minutes or until tender. Stir occasionally.

In a large heat-resistant, non-metallic bowl, crumble the lamb. Heat, uncovered, in Microwave Oven 5 minutes stirring frequently to break up pieces until meat is no longer pink.

Liberally oil a deep, 2-quart, heat-resistant, non-metallic casserole. Line casserole with the reserved eggplant skins. Arrange skins with the purple sides toward the outside and wide ends of eggplant skins at the top of the casserole.

Drain the lamb juices and discard. Add chopped eggplant, onion, mushrooms, the 1 teaspoon salt, thyme, rosemary and garlic to the cooked lamb. Stir to combine well. Heat, uncovered, in Microwave Oven 5 minutes or until onion is tender.

In a small heat-resistant, non-metallic bowl combine beef stock and cornstarch until smooth. Heat, uncovered, in Microwave Oven 1 minute or until thickened and clear; stir occasionally.

Add thickened beef stock with remaining ingredients, except tomato sauce, to lamb mixture. Pour lamb-eggplant mixture into eggplant-skin-lined casserole.

Fold eggplant skins over filling. Heat, covered with a plate, 9 minutes or until a knife inserted in the center of the mixture comes out clean.

Invert onto platter for serving.

Lamb Greats

Serve with tomato sauce.

Chapter 2
N–Z

NARGIS KOFTA – BOILED EGGS WRAPPED IN SPICY MEAT –N. INDIA

1 servings
Source: Lamb Greats

- ¾ lbs. **finely ground lamb**
- 2 tablespoons **coriander leaves, finely chopped**
- 1 teaspoon **salt**
- 3 **hot green chilies, finely chopped**
- 3 **cloves garlic, minced**
- 3 tablespoons **onions, finely chopped**
- 3 tablespoons **lemon juice**
- 1 **egg, beaten**
- 4 **hard-boiled eggs, peeled**
- **oil for deep frying**

Mix ground meat well with coriander, salt, chilies, garlic, onion, lemon juice and beaten egg. Divide into 4 portions. Take 1 portion and wrap it around an egg, making sure no hole appear. Deep fry over medium high heat for 4–5 minutes until nicely browned. Cut in half lengthwise to serve.

PAN-BROILED LAMB CHOPS

2 servings
Source: Lamb Greats

Lamb Greats

2 lamb rib chops, 1 inch thick
Sea salt
Fresh ground black pepper
2 tablespoons **brandy**

Trim lamb chops, cutting away all fat with a sharp knife. Heat a sauté pan or skillet and rub it with some of the fat trimmed from the chops. Place chops in hot pan (the hot pan will sear the surface, making a crust). Turn chops only once (about 2 minutes on each side) and season at the last minute.

Remove chops to a warm plate, pour brandy into pan, and light with a match; the alcohol will take away any fat and leave a wonderful flavor. Stir all juices together, scraping pan. Pour juice over chops and serve hot.

PASANDA KABOB

4 servings
Source: Lamb Greats

500 g boneless lamb fillet
3 ¼ tablespoons **ginger-garlic paste**
3 ¼ tablespoons **raw papaya ground to a paste**
salt to taste
100 g butter

1 teaspoon **garam masala powder**
500 cream
2 teaspoons **white pepper powder**
3 bread slices.

Cut lamb into 2.5 cm. to four cm. wide pieces and beat until well flattened with a meat mallet (steak hammer). Mix half of the ginger-garlic paste, papaya paste and salt. Apply it to the lamb pieces and marinate the lamb for about an hour.

Melt butter in a frying pan, add the remaining ginger-garlic paste and garam masala powder. Fry until well browned. Add the marinated lamb pieces, fry well and cook until done. Add cream and white pepper powder, and cook until almost dry.

Cut the bread slices into strips and toast until done.

Garnish the kabobs with toasted bread fingers.

PEPPER-STUFFED LAMB WITH GARLIC CHEVRE SAUCE

8 servings
Source: Lamb Greats

- 2 **Red Or Green Bell Peppers**
- 6 lbs. **Leg Of Lamb, Boned And Butterflied**
- **Salt And Freshly Ground Black Pepper To Taste**
- ¾ cups **Sun Dried Tomatoes In Oil, Drained (About 4-1/2 Oz.)**
- ¾ cups **Olive Oil**
- 2 tablespoons **Minced Fresh Rosemary Leaves**
- 2 tablespoons **Minced Fresh Thyme Leaves**
- 3 **Cloves Garlic, Minced**
- 1 teaspoon **Tabasco Pepper Sauce**

GARLIC CHEVRE SAUCE oz Chevre (Goat Cheese) Cloves Garlic, Minced 1/2 c Light Cream Or Half-and-Half 1/4 ts Tabasco Pepper Sauce Sprig Rosemary

This is exceptional dinner party fare, impressive-looking and superb tasting, flavored with herbs, sun-dried tomatoes, Tabasco sauce, garlic and chevre. To Roast the peppers: Preheat the broiler. Slice the peppers in half lengthwise, and core and seed. Lay the pieces skin side up in a shallow broiling pan and set the pan 3 inches below the heat. Broil the peppers until the skin blisters and turns black. Remove the peppers to a plastic bag and close it; let them steam for 15 minutes. When they are cool enough to handle, peel off the skin.

Place the lamb skin side down on a cutting board or other surface and it dry. Sprinkle the meat with salt and pepper. Arrange the tomatoes and roasted peppers down the center of the lamb, then roll up the lamb, secure it with twine, and set it in a roasting pan. In a bowl, whisk the oil, herbs, garlic, and Tabasco sauce. Pour the mixture over the lamb, turning once to coat. Cover and refrigerate for 24 hours, turning once or twice.

Preheat oven to 450°F Place the uncovered roast in the oven and immediately reduce the heat to 325°F Cook the lamb for minutes per pound, about 2 hours, or until a meat thermometer registers 125°F for rare or 140°F for medium. Let the lamb stand for 15 minutes before slicing. Meanwhile, in a small saucepan over low heat, whisk together the chevre, garlic, cream, and Tabasco sauce until the mixture is well blended and heated thoroughly. Garnish with rosemary and serve with the lamb.

QUICK CASSOULET

12 servings
Source: Lamb Greats

- 1 ½ lbs. **pork shoulder**
- 2 lbs. **lamb shoulder**
- 2 tablespoons **canola oil**
- 3 **onions, coarsely chopped**
- 10 ounces **beef bouillon**
- ¾ lbs. **polish sausage links**
- 84 ounces **baked beans, 3-28 oz cans**

Trim and cut pork and lamb into 1" cubes. Freeze bones for soup. Brown meat in hot oil. Add onion and stir fry until onion colors. Add bouillon and cover.

Braise on top heat or in oven at 350°F for 1 hour. Add sausage, cut in thick pieces, add a little boiling water and cover.

Add a little boiling water occasionally if necessary. Continue braising for 30 minutes. When meats are tender, remove from heat and stir in beans. Adjust for seasoning if needed.

Possible seasonings-garlic, ketchup, dark sauce, salt, pepper or any seasonings you like.

Freezes well.

RACK OF LAMB, CRANBERRY-TANGERINE SAUCE, BRAISED RED CHARD

4 servings
Source: Lamb Greats

=== LAMB ===

2 racks lamb - (abt 2 3/4 to 3 lbs total)

= (ask the butcher to trim and French)

Extra-virgin olive oil, for drizzling

Coarse salt, to taste

Freshly-ground black pepper, to taste

1 cup **cranberry juice concentrate**

4 **tangerines**, zested and juiced

½ cup **chicken stock**

½ cup **dried sweetened cranberries**

=(Craisins brand name recommended)

=== CHARD ===

1 tablespoon **extra-virgin olive oil**

1 small **onion**, chopped

5 cups **coarsely-chopped cleaned red Swiss chard**

= (the yield of 1 large bunch)

1 cup **vegetable stock**

2 handfuls **golden raisins**

Salt, to taste

Freshly-ground black pepper, to taste

½ teaspoon **freshly-grated nutmeg**

=== POLENTA ===

1 tablespoon **extra-virgin olive oil**

Lamb Greats

- 4 slices **pancetta, chopped**
- 3 cups **chicken stock**
- 1 cup **quick cooking polenta**
- 2 tablespoons **chopped fresh sage leaves**
- 2 tablespoons **butter, cut small pieces**
- **Salt, to taste**
- **Freshly-ground black pepper, to taste**
- 10 blades **fresh chives, snipped or finely chopped**

Preheat grill pan to high and oven to 400°F.

Drizzle racks with oil and season with salt and pepper. Grill lamb over high heat for 2 or 3 minutes on each side. Transfer to a baking sheet or broiler pan and place in hot oven. Cook 12 to 15 minutes, to 130 degrees on meat thermometer for rare, 155 for well. Let meat rest 5 to 10 minutes before serving for juices to redistribute.

For the chard, heat a large skillet over medium-high heat. Add oil and the onion and saute for 2 minutes. Then add the greens in bunches until they wilt down enough to fit in the pan. Add the vegetable stock and raisins. Season greens with salt, pepper and freshly grated nutmeg. Reduce heat to medium-low and cook 10 to 15 minutes until greens are tender and no longer bitter.

Place cranberry juice concentrate and the tangerine zest and juice in a small saucepan and simmer together over low heat for 10 minutes. Strain and return to pan. Meanwhile, combine the cranberries and chicken stock in a bowl. Cover and microwave on high for 1 minute. Let stand 10 minutes to reconstitute the cranberries.

For the polenta, heat a medium saucepan over medium-high heat. Add oil and pancetta. Brown pancetta a minute or 2 and remove from pan to a paper towel lined plate. Return pan to heat and bring 3 cups chicken stock to a boil. Add the polenta and stir constantly until mixture masses, 2 or 3 minutes. Remove polenta from heat and stir in sage, butter, pancetta bits, and season with salt and pepper. Reserve the chives for garnish.

Heat cranberries and stock to a bubble and remove from stove.

To serve, allow 1/2 rack of lamb per person. Separate chops into 1 or 2 rib sections and glaze with cranberry-tangerine sauce. Serve with sage and pancetta polenta garnished with chives and braised red chard.

This recipe yields 4 servings.

RACKS OF LAMB WITH WHITE BEANS

8 servings
Source: Lamb Greats

- **4 racks of lamb, each with 7 or 8 ribs, 3 to 3 ½ lbs. total, Frenched**
- **Salt and freshly ground pepper, to taste**
- ½ cup **extra-virgin olive oil**
- 1 ½ cups **roasting crust**
- 3 tablespoons **Dijon mustard**
- ⅓ cup **minced shallots**
- ⅓ cup **dry sherry**
- 1 cup **chicken stock**
- 4 teaspoons **veal demi-glace**
- 2 tablespoons **unsalted butter, at room temperature**

Preheat an oven to 450°F. Lightly season the racks of lamb with salt and pepper.

In a large roasting pan or saute use pan over high heat, warm 3 Tbs. of the olive oil until almost smoking. Add the racks of lamb and brown on both sides, about 2 minutes per side. Transfer to a carving board.

In a shallow bowl, combine the roasting crust and the remaining 5 Tbs. oil. Brush the meat side of the racks with the mustard, then coat with the roasting crust mixture. Arrange the racks, crust side up, in

Lamb Greats

the roasting pan, spacing them evenly apart.

Roast until an instant-read thermometer inserted into the thickest part of the rack, away from the bone, registers 130∞F for medium-rare, 15 to 20 minutes, or until done to your liking. Transfer the racks to a clean carving board, cover loosely with aluminum foil and let rest for 5 minutes.

Pour off all but 2 Tbs. of the fat from the pan and set the pan over medium heat. Add the shallots and sauté until softened, about 2 minutes. Add the sherry and cook, stirring to scrape up the browned bits, until reduced by half, 2 to 3 minutes. Whisk in the stock and demi-glace and cook until slightly thickened, 3 to 5 minutes, then whisk in the butter. Pour the sauce through a fine-mesh sieve into a sauceboat.

Carve the racks into individual chops and arrange on a warmed platter. Pass the sauce alongside.

Comments: To recommend a wine for this dish, we turned to Karen MacNeil, wine programs chair, Culinary Institute of America, and author of The Wine Bible. Here's what she had to say: "Lamb has a sweet gamelike meatiness that begs for red wine. For these racks, however, not just any red will work. Thanks to the mustard, demi-glace and roasting crust, the flavor ante has been upped. The perfect wine needs to match the lamb's meatiness and intensity and have enough grip to withstand all the dramatic seasoning. My favorite choice: a French Ch,teauneuf-du-Pape or California Rhone blend." Serve these racks of lamb with our warm white bean salad.

REALLY SIMPLE BARBEQUE SAUCE

1 servings
Source: Lamb Greats

1 each onion, finely chopped

2 tablespoons **vinegar**

2 tablespoons **fat or cooking oil**

2 tablespoons **brown sugar**

4 tablespoons **lemon juice**

1 cup **catsup**

3 tablespoons **Worcestershire sauce**

½ cup **water**

½ teaspoon **Tabasco sauce salt to taste**

liquid smoke (optional)

Brown onion in the oil and add remaining ingredients. Simmer for 30 minutes.

Transfer to a blender and thoroughly blend, making a smooth sauce.

Use, for beef, chicken, pork, or lamb.

ROAST LAMB WITH MINT-APPLE COUSCOUS

6 servings
Source: Lamb Greats

For the marinade:

1 cup **dry white wine**

1 **onion, roughly chopped**

3 **garlic cloves, chopped**

2 tablespoons **firmly packed light brown**

sugar

2 **bay leaves**

1 teaspoon **peppercorns**

1 **leg of lamb, about 4 lb.**

1 tablespoon **olive oil**

For the mint-apple couscous:

2 cups **couscous**

4 cups **boiling water**

5 ounces **green beans, thinly sliced**

2 cups **frozen peas**

4 tablespoons **olive oil**

Finely grated zest and

juice of 2 lemons

Salt and freshly ground

pepper, to taste

2 **red sweet apples,**

cored and diced

4 tablespoons **chopped fresh mint leaves**

For the garnish:

Lemon wedges

Fresh mint sprigs

Lamb Greats

To make the marinade, combine the wine, onion, garlic, brown sugar, bay leaves and peppercorns in a large plastic bag.

Rinse the lamb in cold water, pat dry with paper towels and prick with a fork. Add the lamb to the bag and seal well. Put it into a large, shallow container or roasting pan and refrigerate overnight.

Remove the lamb from the refrigerator, turn it over in the marinade and let stand at room temperature for 1 hour.

Preheat an oven to 375°F.

Remove the lamb from the bag and put it in a roasting pan; reserve and refrigerate the marinade. Drizzle the lamb with the olive oil. Cook for 25 minutes per pound for medium plus an extra 25 minutes for well-done, spooning the meat juices over the lamb once or twice during cooking.

About 15 minutes before the lamb is done, make the mint-apple couscous. Put the couscous in a bowl and add the boiling water. In a saucepan of boiling water, cook the green beans and peas for 4 minutes. In a bowl, mix together the olive oil, lemon zest and juice, salt and pepper and stir in the diced apple. Pour off any excess water from the couscous, then stir in the green beans and peas and the apple mixture. Add the chopped mint and toss together.

Transfer the lamb to a carving board and cover with aluminum foil. Pour the juices from the roasting pan into a saucepan, add the reserved marinade and boil for 3 minutes. Strain into a sauceboat to serve at the table. Slice the lamb and arrange each serving on top of some couscous. Garnish with lemon wedges and mint sprigs.

Comments: The natural sweetness of new-season roast lamb is unique. Here it is served with a much lighter and more refreshing alternative to roast potatoes: a warm, tangy couscous salad flecked with diced apple, green beans and peas, bathed in a minty lemon dressing.

Author Note: Note: For a summer version, serve with barbecued butterflied shoulder of lamb. If you are not feeding a crowd, reduce the size of the couscous salad and serve with broiled lamb chops or lamb kabobs.

ROAST LEG OF LAMB

12 servings
Source: Lamb Greats

5 lbs. **leg of lamb**

2 cloves **garlic, sliced**

⅓ cup **olive oil**

1 teaspoon **salt, coarse or Kosher**

½ teaspoon **black pepper, freshly ground**

1 teaspoon **rosemary**

½ teaspoon **thyme**

Trim lamb of fat. Cut slits about 1/2" deep all over lamb and insert slivers of garlic. Rub all over with olive oil. Combine salt, pepper, and herbs and rub herb mixture all over lamb.

Allow to sit at room temperature 20 minutes. Preheat oven to 450°F. Roast lamb for 15 minutes at 450 degrees, then turn oven down to 350°F. Continue to roast until desired degree of doneness is reached, about an hour for medium rare. Baste with pan juices once or twice. Remove from pan and allow to rest at room temperature for 15-20 minutes before carving.

Potatoes, carrots, and onions may be roasted in pan with lamb. Baste occasionally.

ROAST LEG OF LAMB WITH RED PEPPER SABAYON

6 servings
Source: Lamb Greats

3 tablespoons **minced garlic**

1 tablespoon **salt**

1 ½ teaspoons **freshly ground black pepper**

2 tablespoons **olive oil**

1 **bone-in leg of lamb**, 4 to 5 lb.

1 **lemon**, thinly sliced

For the red pepper sabayon:

1 **roasted red bell pepper**, seeded and cut into 1-inch pieces

¼ cup **dry white wine or vermouth**

4 **egg yolks**

4 tablespoons (1/2 stick) **cold unsalted butter**, cut into 8 pieces

½ teaspoon **salt**

¼ teaspoon **freshly ground white pepper**

2 teaspoons **minced fresh mint**

Preheat an oven to 500°F.

In a small bowl, combine the garlic, salt, black pepper and olive oil and mix well. Using a small, sharp knife, cut 10 slits, each about 1 1/2 inches deep, into the lamb. Push some of the garlic mixture into the slits and rub the rest over the outside of the lamb.

Line a roasting pan with aluminum foil, shiny side down, and arrange the lemon slices in a single layer on the foil. Put the lamb on top and roast for 20 minutes. Reduce the oven temperature to 300°F and continue roasting until an instant-read thermometer inserted into the thickest part of the meat, away from the bone, registers 130°F for medium-rare, 30 to 40 minutes more.

Transfer the lamb to a carving board, cover loosely with aluminum foil and let rest for 10 to 15 minutes before carving.

To make the sabayon, in the bowl of a food processor, combine the bell pepper and wine and puree until smooth. Let cool to room temperature. Place the egg yolks in a stainless-steel bowl and whisk in the pepper puree. Set the bowl over but not touching barely simmering water in a saucepan. Whisk until the mixture is thickened and doubled in volume and you can begin to see the base of the bowl as you whisk, about 7 minutes. Whisk in the butter 2 pieces at a time until smooth. Remove from the heat and stir in the salt and white pepper. Fold in the mint. Serve immediately.

Carve the lamb into thin slices and serve on warmed individual plates. Transfer the sabayon to a sauceboat and pass alongside.

Cooking Tip: Variation Tip: To make lemon sabayon, omit the bell pepper in the sabayon recipe and substitute 1 Tbs. fresh lemon juice.

Comments: You can roast bell peppers by holding them directly over a gas flame on a stovetop or placing them in a broiler. Whichever method you use, turn the peppers with tongs until the skin is blistered and blackened on all sides; be careful not to let the flesh burn. Put the blackened peppers in a paper bag, close tightly and let stand for 10 minutes, then peel off the charred skin with your fingers. Slit the peppers lengthwise; remove the stems, seeds and membranes; and cut as desired.

Author Note: Note: This dish contains eggs that may be only partially cooked. They run a risk of being infected with salmonella or other bacteria, which can lead to food poisoning. This risk is of most concern to small children, older people, pregnant women and anyone with a compromised immune system. If you have health and safety concerns, do not consume raw eggs.

ROAST LEG OF LAMB WITH SMALL ONIONS

8 servings
Source: Lamb Greats

1 ounce **pancetta**   (or unsmoked streaky bacon)

Lamb Greats

3 garlic cloves

5 lbs. **leg of lamb, to 6 pounds**

*** **marinade** ***

1 ½ teaspoons **coarse salt**

4 tablespoons **olive oil**

6 **peppercorns, bruised**

*** **fresh herbs** ***

1 sprig fresh parsley

celery leaves, to taste

1 sprig fresh rosemary

2 **fresh sage leaves, (2 to 3)**

2 sprigs fresh thyme

1 sprig fresh marjoram

*** **completing the dish** ***

1 ½ cups **light Italian red wine**

1 lb. **small white onions**

1 teaspoon **sugar**

4 tablespoons **lemon juice**

½ cup **orange juice**

2 tablespoons **unsalted butter**

Chop the pancetta or bacon and garlic. Make a few deep slits in the lamb along the grain of the meat and push little pellets of the mixture into the slits.

Rub the leg with the salt, place it in a roasting pan, and pour over the olive oil. Add the peppercorns and the herbs and leave to marinate for 24 hours in the refrigerator.

Preheat the oven to 350°F.

Pour the wine over the lamb and place in the oven. Baste the meat every 30 minutes or so.

Put the onions in a pan, cover with cold water, bring to a boil, then drain. This makes them easier to peel. Remove the outside skin and any dangling roots, but do not remove any layer of onion or cut into the root; this is what keeps them whole during the cooking.

About 1 hour after you put the lamb in the oven, add the onions. Put the pan back in the oven and continue cooking until the meat is to your liking, basting every 30 minutes or so. A roast this size needs about 2 hours; the lamb will be well cooked, not pink.

Remove the leg of lamb from the pan and set aside to cool while you prepare the sauce. Any large roast should be left to rest for at least 10 minutes before carving, for the juices to penetrate the meat. Lift out the onions with a slotted spoon and put them in a heated dish or bowl.

Strain the cooking juices into a clean saucepan. Skim off as much fat as you possibly can. Heat the cooking juices, and add the sugar and the lemon and orange juices. Taste and adjust seasonings. When sauce is simmering, add the butter in little pieces and let it dissolve, while swirling the pan. Transfer to a heated sauceboat.

Carve the roast at the table and pass around the onions, sauce, and other vegetables. This recipe serves 8.

ROASTED TOMATO AND MINT SALSA

3 servings
Source: Lamb Greats

- 6 large **Roma tomatoes, tops removed**
- 1 clove **garlic**
- 2 tablespoons **lime juice, one Mexican lime**
- 3 tablespoons **olive oil, extra virgin**
- 2 **serrano peppers, minced, with seeds**
- 1 ½ tablespoons **cilantro, minced**
- 3 ½ tablespoons **spearmint, minced**
- ½ teaspoon **lime zest**
- ½ teaspoon **orange zest**
- 1 pinch **salt**

With a comal or black iron skillet over medium-high heat, cook the tomatoes until blackened all over. While still warm, pulse tomatoes with the garlic in a food processor until roughly chopped. Let cool to room temperature and add the remaining ingredients. Mix together and let sit at least 30 minutes before using.

Mark Miller writes: "Ripe red tomatoes roasted on a hot steel comal until the skins blacken are a basic element of many Mexican salsas. The smoky flavor adds a complexity to the taste of ripe tomatoes. Mixing fresh mint as a counterpoint to this cooked flavor creates the combination of raw and cooked which is one of the classic taste motifs of Southwestern cuisine. This salsa goes particularly well with the wild Churro lamb that we serve at Coyote Cafe because it does not mask the Churro's unique taste. It can be served with venison chops, grilled pork, grilled marlin, and that faithful standby, tortilla chips."

Serving Ideas : Goes well with venison chops, grilled pork, or chips.

ROMANIAN JEWISH BEEF SAUSAGES

1 servings
Source: Lamb Greats

- 3 lbs. **lean beef chuck**
- 1 ¼ lbs. **fatty beef, (short ribs or plate)**
- ¼ lb. **beef suet**
- 5 teaspoons **kosher salt**
- 1 tablespoon **coarsely ground black pepper**
- 2 teaspoons **ground coriander**
- 1 pn **ground allspice**
- 1 pn **ground bay leaf**
- 1 pn **ground cloves**
- 1 teaspoon **dry mustard**
- 2 tablespoons **whole yellow mustard seed**
- 2 tablespoons **minced garlic**
- 2 teaspoons **sugar**
- ½ cup **water**
- **lamb or beef casings,**
- **(we use lamb)**

Grind lean beef through food grinder with 3/8 inch plate, fatty beef through 1/4 inch plate. In large bowl, mix ground meat with all other ingredients, except water and casings. Add enough water to allow you to work the spices in, knead till well blended.

Stuff into lamb casings and tie into 5 inch links. Keeps in refrigerator 2-3 days, 2-3 months in the freezer.

ROSEMARY-ROASTED LEG OF LAMB WITH BALSAMIC SAUCE

10 servings
Source: Lamb Greats

- 1 tablespoon **kosher salt**
- 2 teaspoons **freshly ground pepper**
- 3 tablespoons **finely chopped fresh rosemary**
- 2 **garlic cloves, minced**
- **Finely grated zest of 1 lemon**
- 1 tablespoon **olive oil**
- 1 **boneless leg of lamb, 7 to 8 lb., rolled and tied with kitchen string**
- ½ cup **water**
- 2 **shallots, finely minced**
- ½ cup **balsamic vinegar**
- 2 cups **chicken stock**

In a small bowl, combine the salt, pepper, rosemary, garlic, lemon zest and olive oil and stir until blended. Coat the lamb evenly with the rosemary mixture, wrap tightly with plastic wrap, and refrigerate for at least 2 hours or up to overnight.

Position a rack in the lower third of an oven and preheat to 450°F. Let the lamb stand at room temperature for 45 minutes to 1 hour.

Set the lamb on a rack in a roasting pan and roast for 15 minutes. Using large tongs, turn the lamb over, add the water to the pan and roast for 15 minutes more. Reduce the oven temperature to 350°F. Continue roasting, turning the lamb every 20 minutes, until an instant-read thermometer inserted into the center of the meat registers 125°F to 130°F for very rare to medium-rare, about 1 hour more, or until done to your liking.

Transfer the lamb to a carving board, cover loosely with aluminum foil and let rest for 10 minutes before carving.

Meanwhile, pour any juices from the pan into a bowl. Skim off the fat, reserving 2 Tbs., and set the pan over medium-high heat. Add the reserved fat and the shallots and cook, stirring to scrape up any browned bits from the pan bottom, until the shallots are tender, 2 to 3 minutes. Add the vinegar and cook, stirring, until it is nearly evaporated, 1 to 2 minutes more. Add the stock, bring to a boil and cook, stirring, until the liquid is reduced by half, 3 to 4 minutes more. Transfer the sauce to a warmed sauceboat.

Carve the lamb into thin slices and transfer to a warmed platter. Pass the sauce alongside.

Comments: Marinating the lamb for an extended period of time will help tenderize the meat while infusing it with more flavor. The marinade also creates a delicious exterior on the lamb after roasting.

ROYAL LAMB CHOPS BRAISED WITH NUTS AND SAFFRON

2 servings
Source: Lamb Greats

4 tablespoons **unsalted butter**

¼ cup **sliced almonds**

¼ cup **slivered pistachios**

6 large **garlic cloves**

1 one-inch piece **fresh ginger**

1 teaspoon **coriander**

5 **green cardamom pods,** husked

1 **fresh hot green chile**

¼ teaspoon **black peppercorns**

5 whole **cloves**

½ teaspoon **royal cumin, or regular seeds, (see note)**

¼ teaspoon **ground mace**

¼ cup **water**

3 **lamb rib chops,** 4 ounces

trimmed of all fat

½ cup **water**

½ teaspoon **saffron threads, dissolved**

2 tablespoons **hot water**

salt, (optional)

½ cup **peas, fresh or frozen**

2 tablespoons **fresh cilantro, minced**

Heat 2 tablespoons of the butter in a heavy pan over medium-high heat. Add almonds and pistachios; cook, stirring, until light brown, about 4 minutes. Remove with a slotted spoon and set aside.

Combine the garlic, ginger, coriander, cardamom, chile, peppercorns, cloves, cumin, mace and water in a blender and blend to form a smooth paste.

Arrange lamb in a large shallow dish. Rub the spice mixture over both sides of lamb. Cover and refrigerate 30 minutes.

Heat remaining 2 tablespoons butter in a large, heavy skillet over medium-high heat. Add lamb and brown well on both sides. Add 1/4 cup of the water and bring to a boil. Reduce heat, cover, and simmer for 5 minutes. Add remaining water; sprinkle in saffron. Cover and cook until lamb is tender, about 10 minutes. Taste, and add salt, if needed. Stir in peas and cook 5 minutes longer. Sauce should be very thick. Transfer lamb to a heated platter. Stir sauce and pour over lamb. Top with fried nuts and cilantro.

SAFED GOSHT - LAMB STEWED IN COCONUT MILK

4 servings
Source: Lamb Greats

3 tablespoons **vegetable oil**

12 **fresh curry leaves,**

?or 3 **bay leaves**

1 2 inch piece **stick cinnamon**

6 pods **cardamom**

8 whole **cloves**

15 **black peppercorns**

⅓ cup **onion, chopped**

Lamb Greats

- 1 ½ lbs. **shoulder of lamb, cut in 1 1/2" cubes**
- 1 lb. **potatoes, peeled, cut in 1 1/2" cubes**
- 2 medium **carrots, peeled, cut in 3 pieces each**
- ¼ teaspoon **ground turmeric**
- 1 tablespoon **ground coriander**
- ¼ teaspoon **cayenne pepper, or to taste**
- 2 **fresh hot green chilies**
- 1 ¼ teaspoons **salt**
- 1 **14 oz can coconut milk, stirred**

Put oil in a pressure cooker and set over medium-high heat. When oil is hot, put in curry leaves, cinnamon, cardamom, cloves, and peppercorns. Stir once and put in onion. Saute for 1 1/2 minutes or until onion is soft, and put in meat, potatoes, carrots, turmeric, coriander, cayenne, green chilies, salt and 1 cup of the stirred coconut milk. cover securely with lid and on high heat bring up to full pressure. Turn the heat to low and cook for 15 minutes.

Lower pressure with cool water poured on lid and remove lid. Cook uncovered over high heat for 5-6 minutes, stirring gently as you do this. Add remaining coconut milk and bring to simmer. Turn off heat.

SAMOOSA (SMALL SAVORY PASTRIES)

32 servings
Source: Lamb Greats

pastry

- 1 ½ cups **all-purpose flour**
- ¾ teaspoons **salt**
- 1 tablespoon **oil or ghee, (clarified butter)**
- ½ cup **warm water**

filling

- 1 tablespoon **oil or ghee**
- 1 clove **garlic, finely chopped**
- 1 teaspoon **fresh ginger root, finely chopped**
- 2 medium **onions, finely chopped**
- 2 teaspoons **curry powder**

½ teaspoon **salt**

1 tablespoon **vinegar or lemon juice**

8 ounces **steak or lamb, minced**

½ cup **hot water**

1 teaspoon **garam masala**

2 tablespoons **fresh mint or coriander leaves, chopped**

oil for frying

Pastry:

Sift flour and salt into a bowl, add oil and warm water and mix thoroughly, until ingredients are combined. (Add a little more water if necessary to combine ingredients.)

Knead for about 10 minutes or until dough is elastic. Cover with plastic wrap and set aside while preparing filling.

Filling:

Heat oil in a saucepan and fry garlic, ginger and half the onion until onion is soft.

Add curry powder, salt and vinegar, mix well.

Add minced steak and fry over a high heat, stirring constantly until meat changes color. Turn heat down and add hot water.

Cover pan and cook until meat is tender and all the liquid has been absorbed.

Towards end of cooking, stir frequently to prevent meat from sticking to base of pan.

Sprinkle with garam masala and chopped mint or coriander, remove from heat and allow to cool. Mix in reserved chopped onion.

Take small pieces of dough, shape into balls and on a lightly floured board roll each one thinly to a circle, the size of a saucer.

Cut each circle in half. Put a teaspoon f filling on one side of each half circle and brush edges with water. Fold dough over and press edges together firmly.

You will now have triangular shaped samoosas. When they are all made, heat oil in a deep pan and deep fry a few at a time until golden brown on both sides.

Drain on absorbent paper and serve hot. NOTE: Both samoosa and singara can be made using spring roll wrappers. Cut into 2 1/2 inch strips the length of the pastry.

Put a teaspoon of filling at one end and fold the pastry over diagonally, then fold again and again, still keeping a triangular shape.

Moisten end of strip with water or beaten egg and press lightly.

SEALED POT CURRY (SINDHI)

1 servings
Source: Lamb Greats

- 2 ¼ lbs. **lamb or mutton, (it's best with goat)**
- 4 ½ ounces **ghee**
- 7 ounces **yogurt**
- 1 teaspoon **corn flour**
- 7 ounces **tomatoes**
- 9 ounces **onion**
- 1 **garlic bulb, yes bulb not clove**
- 10 **cardamoms, regular**
- 3 **bay leaves, (tejpat)**
- 1 tablespoon **turmeric powder**
- 2 tablespoons **coriander powder**
- 1 teaspoon **salt, up to 2**
- 1 tablespoon **Hungarian sweet paprika***
- 1 teaspoon **chile powder**

Chapter 2: N-Z

* this is a substitution for kashmeri mirch -- (red pepper)

Wash the meat and dry with a paper towel. Clove and skin the garlic and mash with a knife Cream the yogurt with cornflower in a blender for just 5 to 10 seconds- otherwise butter will be released. Sometimes I just whip by hand. Place tomatoes in boiling water for a few minutes to loosen skin. Peel them and slice to 1/5" thickness. Slice onions in medium thickness, 1/4" to 1/3".

Now put everything including the rest of the ingredients into a pot with a flat lid. Seal the lid and pot with dough -- made from flour and water. Place a 2# weight on top.

Cook on slow fire for 50 - 60 minutes. Uncover and test the meat and if salt is ok. If meat is not done cook a little longer. I under salt as my family has become used to a very little salt in our food, but a lot of spice.

Ladle the curry into a serving dish and serve with Basmati rice or nan.

Note: Beef, Pork or venison can be used instead of mutton, lamb or goat. Venison may take a little longer to cook.

You can use a heavy flame proof casserole with a heavy lid instead of sealing with the dough. (such as la Crusset) I have used a Chinese clay pot that can go on the stove/open flame as well.

Special note: The meat used is referred to as goulash cut. In India it is gol boti, meaning circular pieces and a term for curry meat. Anyway, get some nice marbled meat and cube it up!

SEARED AHI TUNA WITH EGGPLANT MARMALADE AND HORSERADISH CREAM

2 servings
Source: Lamb Greats

=== **EGGPLANT MARMALADE** ===

1 **Japanese eggplant**

1 tablespoon **olive oil**

¼ teaspoon **salt**

1 teaspoon **minced ginger**

1 **shallot, minced**

1 clove **garlic, minced**

1 tablespoon **soy sauce**

1 teaspoon **sesame oil**

seasoned rice vinegar

=== **HORSERADISH CREAM** ===

1 cup **whipping cream**

1 teaspoon **minced shallot**

freshly-ground black pepper, to taste

1 tablespoon **prepared horseradish**

red wine vinegar

Salt, to taste

=== **ASSEMBLY** ===

2 pieces **ahi tuna** - (5 oz ea)

½ teaspoon **freshly-ground black pepper**

1 tablespoon **peanut oil**

Eggplant Marmalade: Rub eggplant with 1 teaspoon oil then sprinkle with salt. Set in small pan and roast at 350 degrees until soft, about 20 to 25 minutes. When eggplant is cool enough to handle, peel and chop into small pieces.

Combine ginger, shallot, garlic, soy sauce, sesame oil and splash of vinegar. Saute in remaining 2 teaspoons oil over medium-low heat until fragrant, 2 to 3 minutes. Add eggplant and cook another 2 to 3 minutes. (Makes 1/2 cup)

Horseradish Cream: Combine whipping cream, shallot, pepper and horseradish and cook over medium heat until thick and reduced by 1/4. Add a splash of vinegar and salt and pepper to taste.

Assembly: Coat ahi pieces with pepper. Warm oil in skillet over high heat. Place fish in pan and sear both sides so that fish is browned outside but rare inside, 1 minute per side.

Divide Marmalade between 2 plates. Set fish on top, then drizzle Horseradish Cream around tuna. The marmalade also goes well with meat or lamb and can be used as a spread.

This recipe yields 2 servings.

Each serving: 855 calories; 1,008 mg sodium; 220 mg cholesterol; 74 grams fat; 10 grams carbohydrates; 38 grams protein; 0.50 gram fiber.

SHEFTALIA (BARBEQUE SAUSAGES)

50 servings
Source: Lamb Greats

- 1 ⅛ lbs. **finely ground fatty pork**
- 1 ⅛ lbs. **finely ground veal or lamb**
- 1 **large onion, finely chopped** or- **grated**
- ½ cup **finely chopped parsley**
- 2 teaspoons **salt**
- ½ lb. **panna, (caul fat from pig)**

Combine pork with veal or lamb, onion, parsley, salt and a generous grinding of black pepper. Dip panna into a bowl of warm water for a minute or two, remove and carefully open out a piece at a time, laying it out flat on work surface. Cut with kitchen scissors into pieces about 10 cm (4 inches) square.

Take a good tablespoon of meat mixture and shape into a thick sausage about 5 cm (2 inches) long. Place towards one edge of piece of panna, fold end and sides over meat and roll up firmly. Repeat with remaining ingredients. Thread sausages on flat sword-like skewers, leaving space between them. Number on each skewer depends on their length.

Cook over glowing charcoal, turning frequently. Do not place too close to heat as sheftalia must cook fairly slowly so that the inside is well cooked and the outside nicely browned without being burnt. The panna melts during cooking, keeping the meat moist and adding flavor.

Excessive flaring of fire can be controlled by a sprinkle of water on the coals. Serve sheftalia as an appetizer or a main course.

SHORBA OF VEGETABLES

6 servings
Source: Lamb Greats

2 tablespoons **olive oil**

½ **onion, minced**

1 lb. **beef or lamb stew meat, trimmed of fat,**

and cut into 1/2" cubes

2 teaspoons **sweet Hungarian paprika**

8 **cilantro sprigs**

12 **parsley sprigs**

2 **celery stalks with leaves, finely chopped**

3 **tomatoes, peeled, seeded,**

and coarsely chopped

1 **potato, peeled, and**

cut into 1/4" dice

3 **carrots, cut 1/4" dice**

5 cups **water**

10 **Spanish saffron threads, crushed**

1 **zucchini, cut 1/4" dice**

¼ cup **lentils, rinsed, drained**

¼ cup **crushed vermicelli**

2 teaspoons **salt**

½ teaspoon **freshly-ground black pepper**

Chopped **parsley or cilantro leaves, for garnish**

Tie cilantro and parsley sprigs with cotton string.

Heat oil in large saucepan or soup pot over medium-high heat and fry onion, meat and paprika, stirring occasionally, until onion softens, 4 to 5 minutes. Add cilantro, parsley, celery, tomatoes, potato, carrots and water.

Bring to boil over high heat. Add saffron. Cover and reduce heat to medium-low. Simmer until meat is tender, 45 to 50 minutes.

Add zucchini, lentils and vermicelli. Continue cooking, covered, until lentils are tender, 20 to 25 minutes. Discard cilantro and parsley. Season with salt and pepper.

Ladle soup into individual bowls and sprinkle with chopped parsley or cilantro. Serve immediately.

This recipe yields 6 servings.

Each serving: 242 calories; 853 mg sodium; 31 mg cholesterol; 7 grams fat; 28 grams carbohydrates; 18 grams protein; 2.10 grams fiber.

SLAVONIJA BRAISED LAMB

1 servings
Source: Lamb Greats

3 lbs. **Lamb shoulder cut into 1-inch cubes**

3 tablespoons **Butter or arine**

⅓ cup **Chopped onion**

1 tablespoon **Paprika**

1 tablespoon **Tarragon**

Salt

½ cup **Water or stock**

1 cup **Sour cream**

---SPAETZLE--- Eggs; slighty beaten pn Salt c Flour (about)

Brown lamb slowly in butter, adding additional butter if needed; add onion and paprika. Saute 2 or 3 minutes, then add vinegar, salt and stock. Cover and simmer until meat is tender, about 45 minutes. Stir in sour cream and heat to serving temperature. Serve with Spaetzle or noodles.

SPAETZLE: Mix eggs, salt and flour together to form a fairly stiff dough. Roll out into a rectangle about 1/8 inch thick on a damp breadboard. With a damp table knife, cut into strips 1 inch wide. Cut or pinch off 1 inch pieces and drop into a kettle of boiling, salted water. When the dough comes to the surface, they are done. Drain in a colander and quickly turn into a hot bowl or casserole. Sprinkle with butter or buttered crumbs; toss lightly and serve with any sauced meat dish.

SLOW-COOKER BRAISED LAMB SHANKS

4 servings
Source: Lamb Greats

- 1 yellow onion, diced
- 2 celery stalks, diced
- 2 carrots, peeled and diced
- 3 garlic cloves, crushed
- 2 cups chicken stock
- 1 cup peeled, seeded and chopped tomatoes
- 2 tablespoons tomato paste
- 1 teaspoon chopped fresh thyme
- 1 bay leaf
- 4 lamb shanks, external fat trimmed
- Salt and freshly ground pepper, to taste
- 2 tablespoons olive oil
- 1 cup red wine

Put the onion, celery, carrots, garlic, stock, tomatoes, tomato paste, thyme and bay leaf in a slow cooker and stir to combine.

Season the lamb shanks with salt and pepper. In a large saute pan over medium-high heat, warm the olive oil until nearly smoking. Add the shanks and brown on all sides, about 5 minutes total. Transfer to the slow cooker.

Remove the saute pan from the heat, pour in the wine and return to medium-high heat. Bring to a simmer, stirring to scrape up any browned bits from the pan bottom. Add the wine to the slow cooker, cover and cook on high for 6 hours according to the manufacturers instructions. Transfer the lamb shanks to a large serving dish.

Remove the bay leaf from the cooking liquid. Using a blender or stick blender, puree the liquids and solids until smooth. Pour some of the sauce over the shanks and pass the rest alongside.

Comments: Braised in a slow cooker, these lamb shanks are falling-off-the-bone tender. Serve with buttery egg noodles, mashed potatoes or creamy polenta to soak up the flavorful sauce.

TANDOORI LEG OF LAMB WITH CUCUMBER RAITA

6 servings
Source: Lamb Greats

1 **boneless leg of lamb, about 5 lb., butterflied**

Kosher salt, to taste

1 cup **tandoori grilling paste**

For the cucumber raita:

1 **seedless cucumber, peeled and grated**

2 cups **plain yogurt, store-bought or homemade**

(see related recipe at right)

2 tablespoons **finely chopped fresh cilantro**

1 teaspoon **minced garlic**

½ teaspoon **lightly toasted ground cumin**

1 teaspoon **kosher salt**

Freshly ground pepper, to taste

2 **large red onions, halved and cut into slices 1/4**

Lamb Greats

inch thick serving (optional)
Warmed pita bread for

Generously season the lamb with salt. Rub the tandoori paste over the meat and place in a large sealable plastic bag. Seal the bag and refrigerate for at least 8 hours or up to 24 hours.

Preheat an oven to 375°F.

Remove the lamb from the bag. Roll up the lamb and tie with kitchen string at 2-inch intervals. Place in a roasting pan and roast until an instant-read thermometer inserted into the thickest part of the meat registers 130°F for medium-rare, 1 to 1 1/2 hours.

Meanwhile, make the cucumber raita: Place the grated cucumber between several layers of paper towels and press gently to absorb excess moisture. Transfer the cucumber to a bowl. Add the yogurt, cilantro, garlic, cumin, salt and pepper and stir until smooth. Cover and refrigerate until ready to serve.

Transfer the lamb to a carving board, cover loosely with aluminum foil and let rest for 20 minutes. Meanwhile, put the onions in the roasting pan, set over medium heat and cook, stirring occasionally, until tender, 20 to 25 minutes.

Remove the string from the lamb and carve into thin slices. Transfer the onions to a warmed platter and arrange the lamb on top. Serve immediately with the cucumber raita and pita bread.

Comments: Be sure to purchase a boneless leg of lamb, and ask the butcher to butterfly it. This involves cutting the meat almost all the way through so it can be opened up to lie relatively flat, like a book. After marinating the butterflied lamb, roll and tie it with kitchen string.

TEKKADY ATTARACHI (LAMB CHOPS)

4 servings
Source: Lamb Greats

4 pieces – lamb rib

coconut oil to brush and baste braised lamb

FOR THE FIRST MARINADE

2 teaspoons **chile powder**

salt to rub

8 teaspoons **ginger paste, strained**

4 teaspoons **garlic paste, strained**

½ cup **toddy vinegar**

FOR THE STUDDING

12 cloves

12 cloves garlic

4 sticks cinnamon)

16 black peppercorns

FOR THE BRAISING

oil to baste the legs

20 g ginger

24 curry leaves

5 green cardamom

salt to taste

FOR THE SECOND MARINADE

60 g **yogurt, beaten**

60 g **processed cheese, grated**

¼ cup **cream**

60 g **green peppercorns**

30 g **pachchamanga/kairi, (raw mangoes)**

6 **green chiles, slit, deseeded and chopped**

7 ½ g **mint leaves, chopped**

5 g **coriander leaves, chopped**

FOR THE MASALA

¾ teaspoons **fresh black pepper powder**

½ teaspoon **amchur, (mango) powder**

¼ teaspoon **kasoori methi, (fenugreek) powder**

¼ teaspoon **kebab cheeni, (allspice) powde)**

a generous pinch of black salt

For the first marinade: Forcefully rub – as in massage – the kid/lamb racks with chile powder. Repeat the process with salt, then with garlic paste, ginger paste and finally with vinegar. (Each of these ingredients should be rubbed separately and not as mixture). Refrigerate for 30

Lamb Greats

minutes.

For the studding: Using a cooking needle, stud the fleshiest meat of the rack with garlic flakes and the whole garam masala.

For the braising: Rub the racks with oil and arrange in a roasting tray. Add the remaining ingredients and enough water to cover the racks. Braise in a pre-heated oven (400°F) until the liquor begins to boil. Reduce the oven temperature to 150°F and braise for two-and-a-half hours. Remove and discard the liquor. Brush the racks with coconut oil and keep aside.

For the second marinade: Wash green peppercorns and pat dry. (If using canned green peppercorns, drain the brine and pat dry.) Put all the ingredients, except yogurt, cheese and cream, in a blender and grind to obtain a smooth paste. Mix in the whisked yogurt. Remove and pass through a fine muslin cloth or a fine mesh soup strainer into the bowl. Add cheese and cream and whisk to mix well. Rub the coconut oil-coated racks with this marinade and refrigerate for 30 minutes. (Remove from the refrigerator at least 10 minutes before cooking). Mix all the masala ingredients in a bowl and keep aside.

The skewering: Skewer right down middle horizontally and as close to bone as possible. Pre-heat the oven at 250°F Roast in a moderately hot tandoor for five to six minutes. Remove, baste with olive oil and roast again for two minutes. Or, arrange leg on a mesh of charcoal grill, cover the grill and roast over moderate heat for seven to eight minutes, turning occasionally. Uncover, baste with cooking oil and roast again for two more minutes, turning once. Alternatively, arrange leg on a greased roasting tray and put in a pre-heated oven for eight minutes, turning occasionally. Baste with oil and roast again for three more minutes, turning once. Remove.

Baste racks with butter, arrange on carving platter. Sprinkle the mixed masala over the racks. Serve hot.

Chapter 2: N–Z

TURKARI PALAAK MOLEE

6 servings
Source: Lamb Greats

2 tablespoons **oil or ghee**
2 medium **onions** sliced thinly
60 **garlic, crushed**
1 2 inch piece fresh **ginger** finely chopped
1 ½ teaspoons **turmeric**
2 teaspoons **chili powder**
½ teaspoon **ground black pepper**
½ teaspoon **ground fenugreek**
2 teaspoons **ground coriander**
1 teaspoon **ground cumin**
2 teaspoons **hot paprika**
1 kg **lean diced lamb** (2.2 lb) or **chicken**
800 **coconut cream** (1 qt)
1 ½ teaspoons **salt**
2 **curry leaves** (optional)
1 package frozen chopped **spinach**

Heat oil in heavy pan. Add onions and fry until golden brown. Add garlic, ginger and all spices except salt. Fry for 5 minutes until fragrant. If mixture is too dry add a little water.

Stir regularly to prevent burning. Add lamb and toss through to coat with onion/spices. Fry further 10 minutes, stirring to prevent burning/sticking.

Add thawed spinach and mix thoroughly. Add coconut cream and salt. Stir well. Add curry leaves, bring to a rapid boil.

Reduce heat and allow to simmer for at least 1.5 hours covered.

Remove lid and simmer till sauce reduces, usually 15–30 minutes.

This is an exceptionally hot curry, if you prefer a milder curry reduce by half the following ingredients: chile powder and hot paprika.

This recipe also lends itself to substituting chicken for the lamb.

YANKEE LAMB STEW

6 servings
Source: Lamb Greats

3 lbs. **Lamb shoulder cut into 2-in cubes**

½ teaspoon **Salt, or to taste**

Freshly ground black pepper as desired

4 tablespoons **Vegetable oil**

1 md **Onion, quartered**

4 md **Carrots, peeled and cut into 1/2-in rounds**

2 **Celery stalks cut into 4 pieces**

1 tablespoon **Finely minced garlic**

2 tablespoons **Tomato paste**

¼ cup **All-purpose flour**

1 cup **Dry white wine**

5 cups **All-purpose stock OR low-sodium chicken broth**

½ tablespoon **Whole black peppercorns**

2 tablespoons **Chopped fresh thyme leaves**

=OR=-

1 teaspoon -**Dried thyme**

1 md **Potato, peeled and cut into 1/2-in cubes**

2 tablespoons **Unsalted butter**

2 md **Turnips, peeled and cut into 1/2-in cubes**

½ cup **Peas**

PREHEAT OVEN TO 325°F. the meat dry and sprinkle with salt and pepper as desired. Heat the oil in a large covered casserole or Dutch oven over high heat on top of the stove. Add the meat, without crowding, in batches if necessary, and brown well on all sides. Remove pieces to a plate as they are done and reserve. Repeat until all meat is browned. Pour off any remaining fat, and replace the casserole over medium heat. Add the onion, half the carrots, celery, garlic and tomato paste.

Cook 5 minutes, stirring occasionally. Use your spoon to loosen and dissolve the brown bits stuck to the bottom of the casserole. Add flour and cook, stirring, an additional minute. Add the wine and cook for about a minute to burn off the alcohol. Replace the meat (and any juices on the plate) in the casserole and add the stock, peppercorns and thyme. Cover, bring to a boil and place in the oven for 1 1/4-to-1 1/2 hours, or until meat is tender. Meanwhile, combine potatoes, remaining carrots and butter with 1/2 cup of water in a medium saucepan over medium heat and cook for 5 minutes.

Add the turnips and cook, stirring occasionally, until all water is evaporated, leaving the vegetables bathed in butter, about another 5 minutes. Add the peas, remove from the heat and set aside. Remove the casserole from the oven. Using a slotted spoon, remove the meat from the sauce and place it in a bowl.

Pour the sauce through a fine strainer into another bowl and discard the vegetables and spices that remain in the strainer. Replace meat in the pot, add the cooked vegetables and the sauce. Cover and place over medium heat for 5 minutes. Serve piping hot.

Index

" cubes), 73
(1 ml) pepper, 58
(1 qt), 113
(1.5 kg) boneless lamb, 58
(1.5 oz), 34
(1/2 stick) cold unsalted, 92
(10 ml) crumbled dried mint, 58
(15 ml) lemon juice, 59
(2 ml) salt, 58
(2.2 lb) or chicken, 113
(25 ml) olive oil, 58
(255 grams/ 1 3/4 cups), 28
(255 grams/ 2 1/4 cups), 28
(275 grams/2 1/4 cups) butter, 28
(375 ml) chicken stock, 58
(450 grams) boneless, 28
(450 grams/3 1/2 cups) flour, 28
(5 ml) grated lemon rind, 59
(5 ml) ground cumin, 58
(50 ml) dry white wine, 58
(50 ml) pine nuts, 59
(50 ml) raisins, 59
(optional), 69, 77, 113
(or 1 lb of lamb bones), 70
(or two 14 1/4-oz cans diced tomatoes), 70
(or unsmoked streaky bacon), 93
(raw mangoes), 111
(recipe), 78
(see related recipe at right), 109
(we use lamb), 96
(with no bitter white pith), 15
* 1 1/4 cups raisins, 74
* 1 1/4 cups whole, 74
* 1 large onion, 74
* 1 teaspoon ground cinnamon, 74
* 1/2 cup honey, 74
* 1/2 stick (1/4 cup), 74
* 1/4 teaspoon crumbled, 74
* 2 (3-inch) cinnamon sticks, 74
* 2 garlic cloves,, 74
* 2 teaspoons ras-el-hanout*, 74
* 2 teaspoons salt, 74
* 3 cups water, 74
* 3 lb boneless lamb, 74
* 3/4 teaspoon black pepper, 74
* 3/4 teaspoon ground ginger, 74
* accompaniment: couscous, 75
*** completing the dish ***, 94
*** fresh herbs ***, 94
*** marinade ***, 94
butter beans, 64
cheese, 9
dough, 9
for the batter, 44
for the braising, 51, 111
for the first marinade, 50, 111
for the garnish, 52
for the gravy, 51
for the jackfruit, 51
for the marinade, 44, 45
for the masala, 111
for the second marinade, 51, 111
for the studding, 51, 111
jam, 9

Index

lamb, 65
meat, 9
mix for the marinade, 51
mix for the masala, 51
spice paste, 65
***squash,, 9
stuffings, 9
the gravy, 6
the marinade, 6
to braise, 6
- water, 9
--for the meat---, 24
--meatballs---, 75
--sauce---, 75
--vegetables and eggs---, 75
-dried thyme, 114
-warm water, 37
0 g ginger, 27
0 g onions, 27
1 in cube fresh ginger, 46
1 g clove powder, 45
1 oz sliced italian bread, 69
1/2-inch thickness, 63
14 oz can coconut milk, 100
2 in piece stick cinnamon, 46
2 inch piece fresh ginger, 113
2 inch piece stick cinnamon, 99
2 oz sho grain rice, 73
5 g green chiles, 27
5 oz whole new red potatoes, 69
6 oz lean boneless, 68
7" eggplants, 78
= (ask the butcher to trim and french), 85
= (or coarse salt and pepper), 64
= (the yield of 1 large bunch), 85
=(craisins brand name recommended), 85
=== accompaniments ===, 17
=== assembly ===, 104
=== basmati rice ===, 60
=== braised root vegetables ===, 17
=== chard ===, 85
=== colcannon ===, 17
=== eggplant marmalade ===, 104
=== harissa ===, 60
=== horseradish cream ===, 104
=== lamb ===, 17, 85
=== olive tapenade ===, 32
=== polenta ===, 85
=== sephardic charoset ===, 50
=or=-, 114
?or 3 bay leaves, 99
a few drops gulab jal or, 45
a few drops sweet ittar, 45
a few rose petals, 45
a few strands saffron, 45
a few strands saffron,, 7, 52
a generous pinch black salt, 51
a generous pinch of black, 111
a handful of fresh parsley, 17
a knife, 15
a pinch of mace powder, 45
a pinch of nutmeg powder, 45
a pinch of rose petal powder, 51
about 42 cocktail picks, 77
all-purpose, 15, 114
all-purpose flour, 100, 114
allspice, 4, 26
almonds, 45
along the length, 6
amchur, 111
amchur powder, 51
american tablespoons, 28
ancho chilies, 22
and chopped, 60, 70
and chopped into 1/2" dice, 66
and coarsely chopped, 106
and crushed to a paste, 52
and cut into 1/2" cubes, 106
and diced, 50
and drizzling oil, 12
and garnish, 77
and ground, 3
and slightly drained, 37
apple, 50

Lamb Greats

apricot or orange muscat, 56
artichokes,, 58
arugula, 64
as desired, 114
at right), 55
at table, 17
baby artichokes, 57
baby new potatoes, 12
baked beans, 84
balsamic vinegar, 97
bari illaichi, 8
basic tomato sauce,, 57
basil (finely chopped), 3
basmati rice, 60
baste braised, 111
baste braised-, 50
bay leaf, 6, 14, 19, 22, 26, 31, 58, 69, 108
bay leaf) tied with string, 28
bay leaves, 12, 25, 41, 51, 60, 70, 89, 102
beef, 40, 73
beef bouillon, 84
beef or lamb stew meat, 106
beef stock, 12, 22, 67
beef stock or broth, 78
beef suet, 96
black beans, 25
black cardamom, 6, 6, 45, 51
black cardamoms, 65
black olives, 22
black or green cardamom pods, 55
black pepper, 24, 26, 91
black pepper ground, 70
black pepper powder, 6, 44, 45
black pepper to taste, 83
black peppercorns, 25, 51, 98, 99, 111
black), 25
blades fresh chives, 86
blanched almonds, 74
blanched and halved, 6
blanched slivered almonds, 1
boiling water, 22, 41, 46, 89

bok choy, 48
bone from a leg of lamb, 70
bone-in leg of lamb, 67, 92
boneless lamb, 27, 45, 48
boneless lamb fillet, 82
boneless lamb shoulder or beef tri-tip, 41
boneless lamb shoulder,, 15, 39
boneless leg of lamb, 62, 63, 97, 109
boneless stewing beef or, 5
bottle full-bodied red wine, 21
bottle white wine, 1
bouquet garni (thyme sprig,, 28
brandy, 38, 82
bread, 71
bread crumbs, 10
bread slices., 82
broken into large pieces, 37
brown bread, 17
brown onion, 45
brown onions, 42
brown sugar, 88
bulgur, 4
bunch cilantro, 27
bunch italian parsley,, 42
butter, 17, 17, 34, 82, 86, 92
butter beans, 65
butter or arine, 47, 49, 107
butter or margarine, 2, 40
butter), 100
butterflied, 20
butterflied boned spring leg of lamb, 32
butternut squash, 9
cabernet, 14
calabasa, 9
can (14 oz/398 ml), 58
can (15 oz.) chickpeas,, 62
can (19 oz/540 ml), 58
can black-eyed peas, 31
canned tomatoes, 53
canola oil, 84
cans (10 oz. each), 1

Index

cans stewed tomatoes, 31
capers, 32
capsicum red, 42
caraway seeds, 1
cardamom, 6, 6
cardamom pods, 32
cardamom powder, 24
cardamom seeds, 1, 46, 60
cardamoms, 102
carrot, 28, 40, 58
carrots, 1, 12, 19, 41, 60, 106, 108
cashew nut paste, 6
cashew nuts, 45
cassia leaves, 55
catsup, 89
caul fat or crepinette, 3
cayenne pepper, 5, 54, 70, 75, 100
celery leaves, 94
celery seeds, 49
celery stalk, 14
celery stalks, 12, 108
celery stalks cut into, 114
celery stalks with leaves, 106
cheddar or processed cheese,, 6
chicken, 19
chicken breast, 6
chicken breast (2 halves), 36
chicken broth, 14, 31, 34, 56, 114
chicken broth salt freshly, 36
chicken or vegetable stock, 17, 17
chicken stock, 15, 30, 38, 58, 66, 85, 86, 87, 97, 108
chicken stock or water, 55
chickpea flour, 23
chickpeas, 73
chickpeas,, 58
chile powder, 6, 6, 44, 51, 51, 51, 102, 111
chili, 39
chili flakes, 1
chili powder, 8, 24, 26, 40, 53, 113
chilli powder or to taste, 65
chinese sesame oil, 3

chironji, 45
chopped, 6, 6, 9, 73, 86, 100, 100
chopped carrots, 28
chopped chives, 49
chopped cilantro, 60, 71
chopped coriander leaves, 65
chopped flat-leaf parsley, 38
chopped fresh cilantro, 55
chopped fresh cilantro,, 62
chopped fresh dill, 16
chopped fresh flat-leaf, 14, 21
chopped fresh mint, 54
chopped fresh mint leaves, 89
chopped fresh parsley, 32
chopped fresh rosemary, 36, 38
chopped fresh sage leaves, 86
chopped fresh thyme, 14, 108
chopped fresh thyme leaves, 114
chopped garlic, 67
chopped green olives, 71
chopped mixed fresh herbs,, 67
chopped onion, 46, 71, 107
chopped onions, 28
chopped parsley, 31, 69
chopped parsley or cilantro leaves, 106
chopped tomato, 55
chopped walnuts, 50
chopped yellow onion, 55
cider vinegar, 22
cilantro, 95
cilantro sprigs, 70, 106
cinnamon, 4
cinnamon stick, 1, 60, 60
cinnamon stick (2"long), 56
cinnamon sticks, 65
clear lamb stock, 6
clear vegetable stock, 51
clove, 6
clove garlic, 34, 78, 100
cloves, 6, 51, 111
cloves garlic, 5, 40, 51, 58, 81, 83, 111

119

Lamb Greats

cm cinnamon, 45
cm pieces, 43
coarse black pepper powder, 51
coarse salt, 17, 32, 85, 94
coarse salt and freshly, 20
coarse. chopped dried chiles, 3
coarsely chop dried apricots, 56
coarsely chopped, 23
coarsely diced, 1
coarsely ground black pepper, 96
coarsely-chopped cleaned red swiss chard, 85
coconut cream, 113
coconut milk, 41
coconut oil to brush and, 111
cold water, 46, 65
cooked chickpeas, 60
cooked couscous for serving, 62
cooking oil, 48, 53, 65
cored and diced, 89
coriander, 40, 98
coriander leaves, 7, 52, 81, 111
coriander powder, 24, 51, 102
coriander seeds, 23, 46, 61
corn flour, 102
corn freshly cut from the cob, 19
corn oil, 9, 9, 9, 9
corn or peanut oil, 39
cornstarch, 44, 48, 69, 78
couscous, 56, 89
cranberry juice concentrate, 85
cream, 6, 51, 82, 111
crushed, 78
crushed red pepper flakes, 32
crushed through a press, 76
crushed vermicelli, 106
crushed with the side of, 15
cu cauliflower florets, 40
cu eggplant, 40
cubes, 39, 62, 65, 107, 114
cumin, 22, 60
cumin powder, 24
cumin seed, 66

cumin seeds, 23, 46, 60, 61
cup) water, 28
curd, 7, 51, 51
currants, 66
curry leaves, 111, 113
curry powder, 1, 39, 41, 100
cut 1/2" dice, 66
cut in rounds, 23
cut into 1/4" dice, 106
cut into chunks, 17, 60
cut into large, 39
dark soy sauce, 3
desi ghee, 45, 45
dessert wine, 56
dhuniya powder (coriander), 8
diced canned tomatoes,, 12
diced plum tomatoes, 1
dijon mustard, 87
dissolved, 7
drained, 12
drained and quartered, 58
drained and rinsed, 58
dried apricots, 50
dried chili flakes, 34
dried greek oregano, 38
dried hot red chilies, 46
dried mint leaves, 69
dried navy beans, 70
dried oregano, 15
dried red chillies, 65
dried rigani or oregano, 2
dried rosemary leaves, 78
dried small white, 14
dried sweetened cranberries, 85
dried thyme, 69
dried thyme leaves, 78
dry bread crumbs, 32
dry mustard, 96
dry red wine, 15
dry red wine such, 14
dry sherry, 87
dry white wine, 34, 57, 66, 89, 114
dry white wine or vermouth, 92

Index

ds cayenne pepper, 53
ds nutmeg, 36
each onion, 88
egg, 9, 24, 27, 28, 36, 81
egg wash:, 28
egg yolk, 9, 9
egg yolks, 92
eggs, 76, 76, 78
excess fat, 67
extra-virgin olive oil, 1, 12, 14, 38, 61, 66, 67, 85, 85, 85, 87
extra-virgin-olive oil, 64
farmer cheese, 9
fat or cooking oil, 88
fatty beef, 96
fennel seeds, 1, 32
feta cheese (preferably bulgarian), 32
filling, 100
filling:, 28
fine dried bread crumbs, 77
finely chopped, 74, 75, 75, 76, 81, 113
finely chopped coriander, 46
finely chopped fresh cilantro, 109
finely chopped fresh ginger, 1
finely chopped fresh rosemary, 97
finely chopped garlic, 3
finely chopped ginger, 3
finely chopped onion, 73, 78
finely chopped parsley, 105
finely grated zest and, 89
finely grated zest of 1 lemon, 97
finely ground fatty pork, 105
finely ground lamb, 81
finely ground veal or lamb, 105
finely minced garlic, 54, 114
finely-chopped fresh rosemary, 32
firmly packed light brown, 89
flat-leaf parsley, 30
flour, 9, 31, 34, 38, 44, 66
flour for dredging, 15
fluid, 28, 28
fluid ounces oz yoghurt, 73

for serving, 1, 63
for soaking the pulses, 73
for the cucumber raita:, 109
for the garnish:, 89
for the marinade:, 89
for the meat stew, 73
for the mint-apple couscous:, 89
for the red pepper sabayon:, 92
fresh asian or reg., 3
fresh basil leaves, 51, 51
fresh black pepper powder, 111
fresh cilantro, 99
fresh cilantro leaves,, 23
fresh curry leaves,, 99
fresh ginger, 24
fresh ginger root, 100
fresh ground black pepper, 82
fresh hot green chile, 98
fresh hot green chilies, 23, 100
fresh lemon juice, 38, 62, 71
fresh lima beans, 19
fresh mint, 30
fresh mint or coriander, 101
fresh mint sprigs, 89
fresh or 1/2 dry bay leaf, 34
fresh or grated nutmeg, 17
fresh rosemary sprigs, 67
fresh sage leaves, 94
fresh thyme leaves, 34
fresh tomato puree, 51
freshly ground black pepper, 2, 5, 24, 54, 92, 114
freshly ground pepper, 12, 21, 97
freshly ground pepper,, 1, 62, 67, 77, 109
freshly ground white pepper, 92
freshly-chopped, 57
freshly-cracked black pepper, 32, 36
freshly-grated nutmeg, 85
freshly-ground black pepper, 17, 17, 30, 32, 38, 41, 50, 70, 85, 85, 86, 104, 104, 106

Lamb Greats

freshly-ground black pepper,, 57, 60, 60, 66
fried onion paste, 51
from 1 lemon, 15
frozen peas, 89
full-bodied red wine, 12
gaeta olives, 57
garam masala, 27, 101
garam masala (see related, 55
garam masala powder, 44, 82
garlic, 22, 24, 30, 32, 32, 70, 72, 91, 95, 104, 113
garlic bulb, 102
garlic clove, 26, 34
garlic cloves, 2, 14, 36, 37, 39, 43, 57, 59, 60, 62, 89, 94, 97, 108
garlic cloves crushed, 42
garlic cloves minced, 70
garlic head, 38
garlic paste, 6, 6, 8, 44, 44, 51, 51, 65, 111
garnish, 21, 62
garnish (optional), 54
ghee, 6, 46, 102
ghee -, 51
ginger, 26, 39, 43, 51, 55, 111
ginger ground, 70
ginger paste, 6, 6, 8, 44, 44, 51, 51, 65, 111
ginger root, 5
ginger-garlic paste, 82
golden raisins, 1, 60
good teaspoons cumin seed, 28
grape leaves - (16-oz jar), 30
grated, 6
grated gingerroot, 48
grated lemon zest, 30
green beans, 89
green bell pepper, 66
green cardamom, 45, 51, 111
green cardamom pods, 98
green cardamom powder, 52
green cardamoms, 25

green chile, 6
green chiles, 40, 111
green peppercorns, 111
green peppers, 19, 53
grill seasoning, 64
ground, 36
ground allspice, 50, 56
ground beef, 30
ground beef or lamb, 9
ground beef or lamb,, 23
ground black pepper, 36, 113
ground cinnamon, 9, 15, 24, 39, 77
ground cloves, 1, 16, 24
ground cooked lamb, 49
ground coriander, 39, 54, 55, 56, 65, 96, 100, 113
ground cumin, 40, 54, 56, 60, 65, 70, 72, 77, 113
ground fenugreek, 113
ground ginger, 32, 41, 56, 61, 75
ground ginger), 24
ground lamb, 3, 30, 76
ground lamb or beef, 4
ground lamb or ground beef, 75
ground mace, 98
ground pepper, 21
ground quite fine, 23
ground thyme, 17
ground to a paste, 82
ground turmeric, 55, 65, 100
h ale or beer, 69
haldi powder (turmeric), 8
half a lemon, 65
halved, 62
handfuls golden raisins, 85
hard-boiled eggs, 81
head dark curly kale, 17
heads of garlic, 67
herbes de provence, 21
honey, 43, 59, 66
hot green chilies,, 81
hot paprika, 66, 113
hot water, 2, 47, 99, 101

Index

hungarian sweet paprika*, 102
in a little lukewarm water, 7
in oil, 83
inch cinnamon stick, 6
inch thick, 110
inch-diced pork shoulder, 19
instant chicken bouillon, 48
instant minced garlic, 31
into 1-inch cubes, 55
italian tomatoes, 26
jackfruit and greasing the, 51
jalapeno, 26
jam, 10
japanese eggplant, 104
juice of 1 lemon, 54
juice of 2 lemons, 89
juice of on lemon, 24
kashmiri mirch powder, 45
kasoori methi, 111
kasoori methi powder, 51
kathael, 51
kebab cheeni, 51, 111
keep bones for stock), 28
kewra essence, 45
kidney fat, 45
kosher salt, 96, 97, 109, 109
lamb, 5, 8, 42, 43, 65, 66, 68, 111
lamb bones, 25
lamb bones from the meat, 28
lamb chops, 44, 64
lamb cut into 2" cubes, 46
lamb leg, 34
lamb or beef casings,, 96
lamb or beef stock, 42
lamb or chicken, 24
lamb or mutton, 102
lamb or mutton (from, 28
lamb rib chops, 82, 98
lamb riblets, 31
lamb shanks, 1, 12, 14, 22, 34, 108
lamb shanks (3-4 lbs, 56
lamb shoulder, 26, 59, 84
lamb shoulder cut into, 107, 114

lamb stock or beef stock, 75
lamb,breast of or rib chops, 36
large carrots, 14
large dried figs, 16
large fennel bulb, 1
large fleshy lamb shanks, 57
large fresh mushrooms, 72
large garlic cloves, 12, 20, 98
large garlic cloves peeled, 46
large garlic cloves,, 15, 76
large onion, 4, 105
large onions, 5, 24
large red onions, 109
large roma tomatoes, 95
large spanish onion,, 66
large sweet onion, 72
large yellow onion,, 15
laung, 8
lean beef chuck, 96
lean boneless leg of lamb, 71
lean diced lamb, 113
lean ground lamb, 50, 69, 78
lean inch-diced stewing beef, 19
lean lamb shoulder, 55
leaves, 76, 101
leaves only, 42
leaves,, 76
leg of lamb, 2, 20, 38, 83, 89, 91, 94
leg of lamb -, 36
leg of lamb--slit, 6
leg or shoulder of, 65
lemon, 31, 92
lemon juice, 44, 46, 49, 51, 60, 81, 89, 94
lemon wedges, 89
lemon wedges for garnish, 63
lemon wedges for squeezing, 77
lemon zest, 67
lemons, 2
lentils, 106
lg cooking apple, 47
lg onion, 56
light italian red wine, 94

123

Lamb Greats

light soy sauce, 3
lightly toasted ground cumin, 109
lime juice, 95
lime zest, 95
liquid smoke (optional), 89
loin lamb chops, 17
loin lamb chops or, 54
loosely, 76
loosely packed fresh mint, 76
low sodium chicken broth, 69
mace, 52
madeira, 67
marjoram, 26
marmite, 47
matza meal*, 36
matzot;regular,, 37
mawa, 45
mayonnaise, 49
md carrots, 114
md onion, 68, 114
md potato, 114
md turnips, 114
md white onions, 22
meat, 55
medium (2 cups) onion,, 9
medium carrots, 100
medium onion, 30, 53
medium onion chopped, 8
medium onions, 9, 65, 100, 113
medium red bell pepper, 72
medium to large all-purpose potatoes, 17
medium yellow bell pepper, 72
medium zucchini, 72
melon seeds, 45
mexican hard sauce, 22
middle neck of lamb, 47
milk, 25
minced, 39
minced fresh coriander, 3
minced fresh flat-leaf, 12
minced fresh mint, 92
minced fresh parsley, 71

minced fresh rosemary, 12
minced fresh rosemary leaves, 83
minced fresh thyme, 12
minced fresh thyme leaves, 83
minced garlic, 32, 55, 92, 96, 109
minced ginger, 104
minced shallot, 104
minced shallots, 87
mint leaves, 6, 7, 69, 111
mint sprigs (optional), 56
mixed herbs, 47
moroccan oil-cured olives, 32
mung beans, 73
mustard seed, 41
mutton, 28
naan or other flatbread, 63
nectarines,, 34
oil, 5, 8, 25, 50, 51, 51
oil for basting the legs, 51
oil for deep frying, 44, 51, 81
oil for frying, 27, 101
oil or ghee, 100, 100, 113
oil to baste the leg, 6
oil to baste the legs, 111
oil-packed, 21
okra, 31
olive oil, 26, 30, 32, 32, 36, 38, 38, 42, 54, 60, 60, 60, 70, 75, 76, 78, 83, 89, 89, 91, 92, 94, 95, 97, 104, 106, 108
olive oil to brush and, 50
olive tapenade, 32
olivier parmesan dipping, 12
one-inch piece fresh ginger, 98
onion, 17, 19, 28, 34, 40, 75, 75, 89, 99, 102, 106
onion chopped fine, 69
onions, 7, 26, 41, 51, 58, 70, 81, 84
or butternut squash,, 55
or lamb stock, 28
or- grated, 105
orange juice, 94
orange zest, 95

Index

oregano, 22
ounces (175 milliliters/3/4, 28
ounces (300 milliliters/, 28
oyster sauce *, 48
pachchamanga/kairi,, 111
package dry yeast, 9
package frozen chopped, 113
package frozen sliced, 31
package onion soup mix, 34
packaged baby carrots, 17
packed fresh flat-leaf, 76
pancetta, 93
pandan, 52
panna, 105
paprika, 5, 49, 60, 107
parsley, 14, 21, 37, 76
parsley for garnish, 12
parsley sprigs, 26, 70, 106
parsley stalks and small, 28
pastry, 100
pastry:, 28
patthar ka phool powder, 7
peaches, 34
peanut oil, 104
peas, 76, 99, 114
peas), 73
pecorino, 43
peeled, 14, 55, 108
peeled and chopped fresh, 39
peeled and grated fresh, 55
peeled garlic cloves, 1
peeled onion, 47
pepper, 4, 9, 12, 14, 15, 26, 28, 63, 71, 75, 87, 89, 108
peppercorns, 61, 89, 94
piece pumpkin, 55
pieces, 55, 92, 92, 114
pieces – lamb rib, 111
pieces ahi tuna – (5 oz ea), 104
piloncillo,, 22
pimiento strips, 49
pinch salt, 95
pine nuts, 48

pistachios,, 6
pitted and coarsely chopped, 34
pitted dates, 50
pitted oil-cured olives,, 21
plain yogurt, 5, 39, 109
plums, 35
plus extra for, 21
plus more for, 62
plus more,, 77
pn ground allspice, 96
pn ground bay leaf, 96
pn ground cloves, 96
pn of saffron, 1
pn saffron threads, 60
pn salt, 28, 28
pods cardamom, 99
polish sausage links, 84
poppy seed, 46
poppy seeds, 45
pork shoulder, 84
potato, 40, 106
potatoes, 19, 43, 47, 60, 100
powdered dill, 73
prepared horseradish, 104
prepared mint jelly, 64
prepared store-bought irish soda bread or, 17
processed cheese, 51, 111
quick cooking polenta, 86
rack lamb, 50
racks, 50
racks lamb – (abt 2 3/4 to 3 lbs total), 85
racks of lamb, 87
raisins, 22
raita potato salad for, 63
raw papaya, 82
raw papaya paste, 6, 44, 45
raw red onion, 45
recipe, 55
red bell peppers,, 60
red chiles, 27
red kidney beans, 73

Lamb Greats

red onion, 76
red or green bell peppers, 83
red pepper, 19, 73
red pepper flakes, 70
red sweet apples,, 89
red wine, 6, 108
red wine vinegar, 12, 51, 71, 104
rice, 25
rice wine or dry sherry, 3
rinsed and drained, 62
ripe tomatoes, 19
roasted, 60
roasted chana, 45, 45
roasted red bell pepper,, 92
roasting crust, 87
roasting tray, 51
rolled and tied, 15
romaine lettuce, 22
rose petal powder, 7
rose petals, 6, 51
rosemary, 67, 91
rosemary leaves, 57
royal cumin, 98
rutabaga, 17
saffron, 66
saffron strands, 25
saffron threads, 46, 74, 99
salt, 1, 2, 3, 4, 5, 6, 9, 12, 17, 17, 24, 25, 30, 31, 38, 39, 41, 46, 50, 54, 55, 57, 60, 60, 60, 61, 66, 67, 69, 69, 72, 73, 73, 75, 75, 77, 78, 78, 81, 85, 86, 91, 92, 92, 99, 100, 100, 101, 102, 104, 104, 105, 106, 107, 111, 113, 114
salt – (to 4 tspns), 70
salt according to taste, 8
salt and freshly ground, 12, 14, 15, 28, 63, 83, 87, 89, 108
salt and pepper, 47
salt as needed, 26
salt or to taste, 51, 65
salt to rub, 111

salt to taste, 6, 7, 24, 27, 44, 44, 45, 51, 51, 51, 82, 111
sauce, 43
sauvignon or chianti, 14
scallions, 17, 69
sea salt, 36, 82
seasoned rice vinegar, 104
see * note, 57, 58
seeded and cut into, 92
seedless cucumber, 109
seedless raisins, 47
seeds, 60
serrano peppers, 95
serving, 63
serving (optional), 110
sesame oil, 104
shallot, 64, 104
shallots, 97
sherry, 43
sherry vinegar, 66
shortening, 41
shoulder, 74
shoulder cut into 4cm pcs, 42
shoulder lamb chops, 53
shoulder of lamb, 100
shoulder or leg roast, 58
shredded lemon zest, 14
sichuan peppercorns roasted, 3
sl white bread, 49
sliced almonds, 98
sliced fresh mushrooms, 48
sliced mushrooms, 78
sliced thinly, 113
slices lemon, 30
slices pancetta, 86
slivered pistachios, 98
sm onion, 49
small carrot, 30
small cinnamon sticks, 25
small dandelion greens, 32
small onion, 85
small onions, 69
small red bell pepper,, 6

Index

small red chile, 60
small red or green jalapeno, 39
small rib chops, 54
small white onions, 94
small yukon gold potatoes,, 62
smoked almonds, 64
soaked in lukewarm water, 52
soft polenta with lemon,, 58
softened sweet butter, 17
some for drizzling, 64
sour cream, 107
soy sauce, 34, 104
spanish onion, 57
spanish saffron threads, 106
spearmint, 95
spinach, 113
spinach,cooked, 37
split gram, 27
sprig fresh marjoram, 94
sprig fresh parsley, 94
sprig fresh rosemary, 94
sprig rosemary (optional),, 6
sprigs flat leaf parsley,, 75
sprigs fresh coriander,, 75
sprigs fresh mint, 30
sprigs fresh thyme, 94
squash or potatoes, 76
stalk celery, 28
star anise, 6
steak or lamb, 101
steamed rice for serving, 39
stick cinnamon, 6
sticks cinnamon, 51
sticks cinnamon), 111
stock, 43
stock or low-sodium, 114
stock:, 28
strawberry or grape or prune, 10
strips of peel, 15
substitute, 25
such as, 67
sugar, 9, 9, 9, 89, 94, 96
sun dried tomatoes, 83
sun-dried tomato paste, 60
sun-dried tomatoes, 21
sweet hungarian paprika, 70, 75, 75, 106
sweet paprika, 54, 61
tabasco pepper sauce, 83
tabasco sauce salt to taste, 89
tandoori grilling paste, 109
tandoori paste, 63
tangerines, 85
tarragon, 107
tea pon coriander, 60
the shoulder or leg;, 28
thinly sliced, 15
thyme, 26, 26, 31, 91
thyme sprigs, 26
tied with kitchen string, 97
tins, 28
to taste, 77
to 2 t olive oil, 21
to 4 1/2 lb.,, 15
to 5 t olive oil, 15
to taste, 1, 57, 60, 60, 62, 66, 67, 109
toddy vinegar, 111
tomato, 22
tomato chopped, 8
tomato paste, 14, 15, 55, 70, 75, 78, 108, 114
tomato puree, 65
tomato sauce for moussaka,, 78
tomatoes, 70, 73, 102, 106
total, 87
total) bones cracked, 56
trimmed, 16
trimmed of all fat, 99
turm, 75
turmeric, 34, 41, 113
turmeric powder, 51, 51, 102
uncooked rice, 30, 30
unflavored yoghurt, 46
unpeeled eggplant, 72
unsalted butter, 32, 74, 87, 94, 98, 114

Lamb Greats

unsalted cashews, 46
veal demi-glace, 87
vegetable cooking spray, 72
vegetable oil, 12, 22, 24, 31, 34, 55, 68, 73, 78, 99, 114
vegetable stock, 60, 85
vinegar, 43, 88
vinegar or lemon juice, 101
virgin olive oil, 36, 57
warm water, 65, 100
warmed pita bread for, 110
water, 9, 25, 28, 34, 39, 48, 48, 60, 62, 70, 73, 89, 96, 97, 98, 99, 106
water including the water, 73
water or stock, 18, 107
water to cover, 19
whipping cream, 104
white pepper, 26
white pepper powder, 82
white turnips, 41
white vinegar, 41
white wine, 31
whole, 70
whole black pepper, 8
whole black peppercorns, 114
whole cloves, 25, 46, 65, 98, 99
whole milk, 17
whole salt-packed anchovy fillets, 32
whole yellow mustard seed, 96
wine, 26
worcestershire sauce, 19, 89
x hot cooked rice (opt.), 48
x onions, 34
yellow onion, 14, 39, 60, 62, 108
yellow onions, 1, 12, 60
yogurt, 24, 102, 111
zeera, 8
zest and juice of 1 orange, 1
zest of 1 orange, 32
zucchini, 106

Made in the USA
Lexington, KY
13 December 2013